Moving Money

Moving Money

THE FUTURE OF CONSUMER PAYMENTS

ROBERT E. LITAN

MARTIN NEIL BAILY

editors

BROOKINGS INSTITUTION PRESS
Washington, D.C.

Library of Congress Cataloging-in-Publication data

Moving money : the future of consumer payments / Robert E. Litan and
Martin Neil Baily, editors.
    p.   cm.
Includes bibliographical references and index.
Summary: "Examines trend toward digital means of payment, asking several
questions: How will digital money evolve? What impacts will technologies
such as wireless devices have on payment for goods and services? What other
technologies await consumers? And what will the consumer payments
industry look like in the future?"—Provided by publisher.
    ISBN 978-0-8157-0277-1 (pbk. : alk. paper)
    1. Electronic funds transfers. 2. Payment—Technological innovations. I.
Litan, Robert E., 1950– II. Baily, Martin Neil. III. Title.
    HG1710.M68 2009
    332.1'78—dc22   2009015000

9 8 7 6 5 4 3 2 1

The paper used in this publication meets minimum requirements of the
American National Standard for Information Sciences—Permanence of Paper
for Printed Library Materials: ANSI Z39.48-1992.

Typeset in Sabon

Composition by R. Lynn Rivenbark
Macon, Georgia

Printed by R. R. Donnelley
Harrisonburg, Virginia

Contents

1   Introduction   1
    Robert E. Litan and Martin Neil Baily

2   Payments in Flux:
    Megatrends Reshape the Industry   19
    Vijay D'Silva

3   Innovation and Evolution of the
    Payments Industry   36
    David S. Evans and Richard Schmalensee

4   Consumer Behavior and the Future
    of Consumer Payments   77
    Drazen Prelec

5   The Future of Consumer Payments:
    An Insider's Perspective   102
    Kenneth Chenault

6   Competition Policy Issues in the Consumer
    Payments Industry   113
    Nicholas Economides

7   Keeping Electronic Money Valuable:
    The Future of Payments and the Role
    of Public Authorities   127
    Thomas P. Brown

Contributors   141

Index   143

1 ROBERT E. LITAN *and* MARTIN NEIL BAILY

Introduction

M*oney* is one of those words with multiple meanings. Economists tell us that it serves as a *medium of exchange*, or the way in which actors in an economy pay for goods and services. It also is a *unit of account*, or the device by which prices of those goods and services (think dollars and cents) are determined. It is a *store of value*, a way in which actors can hold their wealth, though in modern financial systems there are typically more productive ways to hold wealth, such as financial instruments or hard assets such as real estate (in which case the value of those assets is expressed in the chosen monetary units).

This book is about money and its use, primarily by consumers in the first sense of the term, as a medium of exchange. More precisely, the chapters in this volume attempt to answer the following questions: Over time what forms has money taken? How are these means of payment likely to change in the years ahead? What, if anything, should policymakers do to facilitate those changes or, at a minimum, to avoid holding them back?

Why do answers to these questions matter? For one thing, the payments industry—governments and the firms that enable payments—is large and important in our economy. As noted in chapter 2, in the United States alone, private sector payments providers generate approximately

We wish to thank Adriane Fresh for outstanding research assistance.

$280 billion a year in revenue. This number does not include the substantial governmental resources that go into making money (coins and printing money) or moving it (checks and various electronic transfers).

Second, it turns out that how we pay for things influences what and how much we buy, and when. As we note below, and as a later chapter discusses in much greater detail, there is a significant psychological aspect to how we pay for things. Other things being equal, people tend to buy more goods or services, and to be willing to pay more for them, under certain circumstances, for instance, if they can pay by credit (credit cards) than with cash or its equivalents (debit cards). How the means of payment evolve, therefore, can influence how economies themselves evolve.

Third, the technology of money and means of payment is fascinating in its own right. Continuing advances in technology—communications and the digital revolution in particular—have shaped and will continue to influence what means of payment are devised. At the same time, however, consumers ultimately will determine which of these technologies they will actually use.

Fourth, the payments landscape is likely to be very much affected by public policies toward payments. Any form of payment requires trust on the part of both the seller and the buyer. No one wants to be the victim of fraud or theft. Government is required to enforce laws against such outcomes. Historically, governments also have had monopolies on the manufacture of money and on the means of its transfer (other than in face-to-face transactions). More contentious is whether, and to what extent, government is also needed to protect the market in private sector payments systems.

The chapters that follow address these and other issues associated with consumer payments. The authors are recognized experts, from both the academic and the private sectors, on payments issues. Initial drafts of these chapters were presented at a conference at the Brookings Institution on September 16, 2008.

We set the stage in this introduction by providing a brief history of money and consumer payments and discussing some of the economic characteristics of payments systems. We then outline some of the broad themes that run through the chapters. In doing so, we concentrate, as most of the chapters do, on payments technologies in use in the United States. Where relevant, however, we draw on experiences from other countries.

Money: A Brief History until the Age of Plastic

For thousands of years, people have used different things as money, replacing perhaps an even longer history of a system of barter, the exchange of different goods or services between buyer and seller. Barter is highly inefficient. What I want, you or someone else must have. There must be a coincidence of wants for barter to work. These happenstances become more costly to arrange as the number of people in an economy grows.

What has counted as money has changed over time. Livestock and foodstuffs probably were the first forms. Early in American history, tobacco was also used in some places in the South, and in fact was recognized as legal tender in Virginia in the seventeenth century. But these perishables had a basic problem: they couldn't be stored without much effort and expense, and they eventually spoiled. People turned to more durable inanimate things like shells and stones to overcome this difficulty, but even these forms eventually eroded in value, either through natural causes or because they were easily debased—with enough effort people could find more of them and thus reduce the value of what was already in place.

Nonetheless, certain forms of money have endured, though each is becoming less relevant for consumer payments in our increasingly digital world. For example, metal coins, in one form or another, have been in use since 700 BCE. Paper monies—more precisely, notes giving their holders rights to receive some form of metal in return—are a more recent innovation, first used by the Chinese in 140 BCE and later by the Romans. Paper monies became popular, however, only many centuries later during the Renaissance in Europe, and then in the American colonies, especially during the Revolutionary War.

But paper monies also have shortcomings. Without regulation or some explicit tie to the amount of a recognized commodity (such as gold), the production of notes can easily proliferate, destroying their value. That is why, in modern societies, governments (through their central banks) now exercise control over the production and distribution of so-called fiat money, money that can be used as a means of payment, a unit of account, and a store of value, but which is not necessarily backed by or redeemable for a given quantity of metal.

There is another drawback to both paper and metal money: it must be guarded against theft and must be transported to be used in exchange. The establishment of banks by Venetian traders as early as the twelfth century solved the storage problem by enabling depositors to place their money for safekeeping elsewhere. The banks would move money by simply changing entries in their account books or issuing bills of exchange, the predecessor to the modern check.

But bank money can lead to other problems. Banks can effectively print money by issuing bank notes, promising the holders the ability to redeem such notes in specie, typically gold or another hard metal. This system of fractional reserve banking arose as banks expanded the volume of their note issues relative to the amount of reserves, or specie, they had on hand. The banks counted on the fact that their depositors would not all want their specie back at the same time.

But what if they did, and banks did not have enough reserves to repay them? Such was the weakness of fractional reserve banking, which in fact was subject to periodic depositor runs or panics. In the late nineteenth century and early twentieth, one giant figure of finance—J. P. Morgan—personally used his bank to fight off such panics. Yet one man alone could not be expected to support an entire banking system, and so, in 1913, Congress created a government-controlled central bank to meet the liquidity needs of individuals and firms throughout the economy. The Federal Reserve System (Fed), governed by a central board in Washington, was given authority to establish reserve requirements for banks, to buy and sell government bonds and thereby exercise control over the money supply (although banks' willingness to lend also influenced how much money was in the system at one time), and, if necessary, to serve as a lender of last resort to the banking system.

It is now widely recognized that the Fed failed in discharging two of these responsibilities during the Great Depression, by allowing the money supply to shrink rather than continue to expand, and by not providing enough liquidity to prevent depositor runs that ultimately brought down roughly 9,000 of the nation's banks. Central banks here and elsewhere throughout the world have learned much since then. Although debate continues as to the Fed's role in contributing to the housing bubble that led to the 2007–08 financial crisis and ensuing recession, few have argued with the Fed's massive show of financial force in responding to the events: expanding the money supply at a rapid clip and lending not only to banks with liquidity problems, but to nonbanks and to the commercial paper market as well.

The Fed was given authority not only for managing the nation's money supply but also for clearing checks between banks, which previously had been the domain of private clearinghouses. These clearinghouses had levied the equivalent of small taxes on the checks they cleared to cover the risk that a paying bank would not be able to honor its commitments to payee banks. In 1918, the Fed assumed the risk of nonpayment, meaning that all banks could exchange their checks at par without any discount. In addition, the Fed absorbed the substantial cost of running this clearing operation, which has until recently required the physical counting and movement of an ever-growing volume of checks. Not surprisingly, the check became the dominant payment method in the U.S. economy from the end of the nineteenth century through the twentieth.

That was not the case in Europe, where giro payment systems instead have long dominated. Unlike checks, which put the onus on a payee's bank to collect from the payer's, giro payments put it on the payer, who instructs the bank, which only then transfers the funds to the payee's bank. Direct payroll deposit is an example of how the giro system works: your employer automatically puts funds in your account without writing you a check. Some customers in the United States use similar direct transfers to pay their utility bills and their mortgage or rent, but still often use (again until recently) checks to pay other parties. In Europe, individuals rely overwhelmingly on such direct transfers, and only rarely write checks.

Payments Methods: Plastic and Beyond

We avoid getting enmeshed here in the academic debate over why the United States went one way in payments (check) and Europe another (giro), largely because both systems are under assault from continuing technological change—the leitmotif of this book—which renders the history of how each side of the Atlantic got where it is today increasingly anachronistic. Payments technologies and the industry that has grown up around them have changed dramatically since the end of World War II. The change that launched it all was when money began to go "plastic"—that is, when consumers could pull out a card from their wallets and use it rather than cash or a check to pay for goods and services. This volume takes the plastic era as a given, and explores how the world of payments has moved and will continue moving beyond it.

Actually, the first payment cards were not plastic at all, but paper or cardboard, and limited to certain retailers, such as Sears. What we know today as the general purpose payment card—one that could be used at multiple vendors—began in 1950, when Diners Club launched its card for use at New York area restaurants (later expanded to many other locations). Shortly thereafter, Hilton Hotels introduced the Carte Blanche payment card, for use at hotels. Both of these cards, however, had limited usability, but were notable in how they adopted a two-sided business model: consumers paid an annual membership fee, and merchants paid the payment network a fixed percentage of the amounts consumers paid for the product or service.

American Express and Bank of America changed the payment card industry forever in 1958, when each issued a card that consumers could use at many types of vendors. With a much broader range than either Diners Club or Carte Blanche, both issuers were in a much better position to take advantage of network externalities—the chicken and egg notion that as more users are attracted to the cards more merchants will join, and vice versa. That is precisely what happened. Both American Express and Bank of America's Visa grew rapidly thereafter in popularity.

But the two new players used very different business models. American Express expanded organically, first within the United States, and later throughout the world, adding merchants and customers to its roster, and directly clearing all charges by cardholders and payments to merchants. Bank of America initially tried to expand by franchising, inducing smaller banks to join its network. Eventually, a rival group of banks formed MasterCard, a membership association of banks. Bank of America did likewise, abandoning its ownership of the network in favor of a federation of banks, which became the Visa network. Later, Sears launched its own card network, Discover, eventually spinning it off into a separate business line. Like American Express, however, Discover operated its card network directly, in contrast to the cooperative or membership business model followed by MasterCard and Visa. These contrasting business models coexisted for nearly five decades. In response to litigation over the way in which their members set network fees, both MasterCard (in 2006) and Visa (in 2008) adopted the direct ownership model and became public companies.

American Express's business was also unique in another respect. Whereas the other card networks offered their cardholders credit, for many years the American Express card was only a charge card, which required customers to pay the entire monthly balance when billed. Eventually, however, American Express began to offer credit cards as well so that it could more effectively compete with the other card networks.

Today, credit cards are ubiquitous. In 2007, American consumers charged more than $1.7 trillion in purchases on them ($1.9 trillion in constant 2006 dollars). Outstanding credit card debt topped more than $2.5 trillion, or a median value of $2,200[1] per household that owes money. Having a credit card has become essential to consumers and businesses, even for those who pay their bills promptly (so-called convenience users) and do not use the cards for credit. In many locations, or with many vendors, credit cards serve as personal identification.

In 1975, banks introduced another type of payment card, the debit card. As its name implies, the debit card immediately deducts charges from users' bank accounts. Banks typically have coupled debit card features on their ATM cards, and many now permit credit charges as well. Debit cards historically have been far more popular outside than inside the United States, especially in Europe. But they have been rapidly gaining popularity here despite the fact that users cannot take advantage of the float that credit cards offer (the period between when charges are made and payment of any credit card balance is due). Apparently, many consumers prefer the discipline of spending within their means that debit cards help enforce.[2]

The Internet revolution is now pushing payments increasingly into cyberspace. With Internet banking, customers no longer need to write checks to pay for many routine household expenses, or even to pay off their credit cards. With a few keystrokes on their banks' home page, bank customers can use their computers, tethered to the Internet, to pay bills. European countries with giro systems, meanwhile, have adapted them to the online environment. The Internet also has made possible entirely new payments networks, such as PayPal, that enable individuals to transfer funds either to other individuals or to vendors.

Wireless or mobile payments technologies are the next frontier in payments. In some countries consumers can already use mobile devices such as cell phones to charge payments to their credit card accounts or to debit their bank accounts. In Japan cell phone users are charged directly for the amount of content they download from the Internet. The major payment networks in the United States, along with several new ventures, are working on ways to introduce such services in the American market.

Several characteristics are common to all successful payments technologies or systems. Both the payee and the payer must accept the method of payment, thus forming a two-sided market. Furthermore, payments technologies are not free. Handling money, including the costs of printing it and taking measures to keep it safe (whether at home or in a bank), involves money. It takes money to manufacture, handle, and clear checks. The same is true of the various payments cards: ATM, credit, and debit. Merchants must have card readers and the networks must process the payments transfers (although continued advances in digital technologies have lowered the related processing costs). Mobile payments networks and devices also entail costs. Consumers and merchants balance the relative costs and convenience of the various technologies in deciding which to use.

Nonetheless, consumers display considerable inertia in their use of the various payments methods available. Once consumers and merchants get comfortable with a particular technology, they need a compelling reason to switch to another, as David Evans and Richard Schmalensee explain in detail in chapter 3. As a result, mere incremental improvements in payments technologies typically fail in the marketplace. For a new method of payment to be successful, it must offer substantial numbers of users significant cost savings or added convenience relative to existing payments technologies or methods (although typically younger users have less emotional investment in an existing technology or payment method and are likely to be the most open to try a new one).

Whatever its cost or convenience, a payments system must be trustworthy and secure, or people will not use it. The law can provide comfort to users and thereby accelerate the use of a particular payment method. The federal liability limit of $50 for cards that are stolen or fraudulently used clearly facilitated the rapid growth in acceptability of credit cards. Technology or software code will have to do the same for Internet payments technologies. Payments networks continue to work on a variety of ways to verify users' identity, and consumers surely will see some of them in the future.

These and other themes are covered in the chapters that follow, which we now briefly summarize.

The Future of Payments: A Preview

The next two chapters lay out alternative visions for the future of consumer payments. Vijay D'Silva, a financial services expert with McKinsey and Company, describes in chapter 2 three broad trends that he believes will reshape the industry.

First, the use of checks and cash, which currently account for about half of all U.S. payments transactions, will continue to decline, perhaps at an accelerating pace. D'Silva suggests that the increasing use of electronic payments—clearing of transactions through automated clearinghouses (ACH)—will drive this trend more than the continued growth of payments cards. The progressive digital imaging of checks will reinforce the declining use of paper-based checks, in particular. Under legislation enacted by Congress in 2004, banks are required to honor digital checks in lieu of paper ones. This Check 21 initiative is increasingly driving merchants and banks to image checks. By 2010, D'Silva expects paper checks to have largely disappeared from the banking system.

Second, D'Silva forecasts increased use of payments systems based on open networks, which, in contrast to closed systems, permit users to access a network with their own devices, as long as the devices are compatible with the rest of the system. For example, payments providers are currently experimenting with credit-card-like machines that would allow consumers to directly access ACH networks without having to go through commercial banks. The Internet also may enable other plug-and-play capabilities that will facilitate payments innovations. At the same time, however, the consolidation of the banking industry—especially in the wake of the 2007–09 financial crisis—is likely to drive many more transactions to be processed internally within fewer large banks, because both the payer and the payee are increasingly likely to have banking relationships with the same institution.

Third, D'Silva expects to see many new payments instruments offered by new entrants into the payments industry. Already, mobile wallets are in use in Japan, permitting users to transfer funds to merchants by their cell phones. Transportation authorities in the United States and elsewhere around the world are increasingly mandating "contactless payments" devices, such as E-ZPass transponders in automobiles, which permit drivers to pay highway tolls without stopping at toll booths. D'Silva suggests that a future growth market will be one that provides person-to-person payments across national borders—a more extensively international PayPal. At the same time, D'Silva notes that the payments sector is littered with failed experiments, and he expects the future to be no different in this regard.

D'Silva closes with advice for would-be entrants into the payments industry: be aware that consumer payments behavior changes slowly; adopt a long-run mentality; leverage an existing infrastructure where possible; new payments methods must offer much more than incremental improvements over current methods; and banks are ideal partners because they are key to the payments business.

In chapter 3, David Evans of University College in London and the University of Chicago Law School and Richard Schmalensee of MIT, authors of the leading book on the credit card industry,[3] offer related thoughts about how they see the payments industry and payments technologies evolving. They second the warning of D'Silva that consumer behavior in this area is difficult (and costly) to change, and thus stress that forecasting what the future will look like also is difficult. For this reason, they counsel government policymakers to heed the Hippocratic warning "Do no harm" in setting policy governing payments, given that preemptive rules can have unintended undesirable consequences.

The authors begin with an overview of payment cards, how they arose, and the benefits they have delivered to users. Of particular relevance, the authors lay out the economics of payment cards and the two-sided platform they create. Once consumers and merchants become accustomed to using the platform, they are reluctant to use other platforms or payments technologies. This has not stopped technological progress in payments, however. To the contrary, the revolution in computer and information technology has radically changed the cost and convenience of payments cards over time. Many younger consumers may not realize it, but anyone older than forty must surely be aware that the time it takes for a merchant to complete a card transaction has dramatically declined over the past several decades. Based on the authors' survey evidence, consumers today are quite happy with their payment cards, and show little inclination to use other payments technologies, such as contactless cards or mobile phones. Similar survey evidence for merchants is lacking, but apart from wanting to pay lower merchant fees to the card networks, merchants too have shown little inclination to embrace other payments technologies.

For new payments technologies to succeed they must crack what Evans and Schmalensee call the chicken and egg problem, the notion that consumers won't use a technology unless it is widely accepted among many merchants, and merchants won't invest in accepting payments using that technology unless many consumers are already using it. The authors provide a brief history recounting the failure of a number of innovative payments technologies to solve this problem. One successful exception to the pattern of failures is BillMeLater, a technology that permits the consumer at a retail checkout to click a feature that, after approving the customer based on the last four digits of his or her social security number, pays the merchant and bills the customer later.

The authors are skeptical, however, that any future revolution in payments will come simply from making transactions processing faster or cheaper; there is only so much more that can be done. Instead, they suggest that real change will come from the mashup of payments with technologies and business models that lie outside the traditional payment card industry. One such nontraditional business model could be adapted from the online advertising industry, which though in its infancy has been growing rapidly. The authors speculate that as online ads are more effectively targeted to consumers most likely to respond to them, new payments models may be married with online advertising or develop as an outgrowth.

The mobile phone is another technological platform on which new payments systems are likely to be based. After reviewing the development of the mobile phone industry, the authors survey the possibilities and the realities—especially in emerging markets—of mobile payments.

A special attraction of mobile phones is that they can be and are being used not only for payments, but also for multiple other purposes: locating products and services, price comparisons, and devices for accepting targeted advertising. The emergence and growth of "cloud computing" should also promote other payments innovations in the future.

Evans and Schmalensee conclude with some observations on the appropriate policy framework for promoting payments innovation, a topic that other chapters in the book also explore in even greater depth. Their broad message is that though policymakers should be vigilant in protecting consumers from abusive or deceptive practices, especially in a world where retailers and payments system providers have more and easier access to consumer information than ever before, they should also be cautious to avoid stifling continued innovation.

Although it is clear from chapters 2 and 3 that payments systems have continued to evolve and to meet consumers' needs, it is useful to step back and ask, but what exactly do consumers actually want from their payments arrangements? Drazen Prelec of MIT takes up this seemingly elementary but critical question in chapter 4.

Prelec begins with the puzzle that has challenged a number of payments analysts: why have debit cards, which immediately debit consumers' bank accounts at the time of purchase, been growing at such a rapid clip in the United States (passing credit cards in 2006 as the most popular means of payment, measured by transactions volume), when credit cards permit users to have short-term interest-free credit (until balance payments are actually due)? A similar puzzle surrounds the use of prepaid cards.

Drawing on findings from recent experimental research, Prelec's chapter provides some answers to the puzzle. But to appreciate the answers, it is first necessary to understand his basic framework of analysis.

Prelec begins with a simple, but critical, insight: that payment takes some of the glow off consumption. The pleasure or benefit consumers derive from a given item of service is reduced by having to pay for it. A diner will much happier if he or she doesn't have to pick up the tab for dinner with a friend than if he does. In Prelec's terminology, payments exact a moral tax on consumption. Different payments methods affect this moral tax very differently.

For example, prepayment is one simple way for consumers to reduce the moral tax: having paid for the service or item in advance, consumers can make themselves feel better about using it (or eating it, in the case of a restaurant meal). This is not necessarily true, however, for durable goods, whose services are delivered or consumed over a lengthy period. In that case, consumers prefer to buy on installment, or on credit.

But prepayment has its drawbacks: foregone interest on the money spent and that the payment is irreversible. Prelec describes a number of buffering mechanisms that preserve the moral tax advantage of enjoying a good as if it were free, but giving the recipient some flexibility on how the money is spent. Beads at Club Med locations, usable for food and drink, are one example. Frequent flyer miles are another. Prelec explores how various other payment plans also permit consumers to feel as if the marginal cost of using or consuming a product is free of the moral tax. For example, the most popular Netflix subscription plan for DVD movie rentals charges consumers a monthly fee and allows them to have three DVDs at home at any given time. Because the DVDs are prepaid, the marginal cost of watching another movie is zero.

Prelec uses this framework, and specifically the notion of the moral tax of payments, to explain why debit card use has been growing faster than credit card use. For one thing, when consumers pay by credit card, in reality they are only deferring actual payment—that is, deduction from their bank balances—until they receive and pay their credit card bills. The time lag between purchase and actual payment can make the payment very distasteful, given that it comes well after the purchase, and is in a fundamental way disconnected from the enjoyment of using the item or service.

Second, debit cards provide self-control. Evidence from bidding experiments shows that people are willing to pay more for a given item when they can pay with a credit card than with cash. Debit cards thus constrain bidding and spending. Put another way, payments arrangements that reduce the moral tax also make it more difficult for consumers to track and control expenses, and thus eliminating the moral tax would encourage overspending. The challenge in designing future payments mechanisms is to appeal to consumers' desires for self-control but at the same time to also provide convenience and lower costs.

Prelec's analysis serves as a segue to the last three chapters of the book, each of which addresses from a different perspective what policymakers should do to promote payments innovations. In chapter 5, Kenneth Chenault, chairman and CEO of American Express, examines the policy environment through the lens of the history of Amex's own payment cards. That experience teaches two lessons: that change is a constant in the payments business, and that trust is key to its success.

Change is reflected in the current move to online and mobile transactions, as well as by entry of new players—other than the main payment card networks—into the industry (such as Verizon, BillMeLater, and PayPal). Chenault is optimistic that electronic payments products, in particular, will grow in volume, both in the United States and around the world, because of the growing acceptance of these products and continued changes in technology.

No player or payment technology will be used, however, unless both consumers and merchants trust that it will handle transactions correctly, promptly, and efficiently. Yet, as Chenault candidly notes, public confidence in the credit card segment of the payments industry has eroded in recent years in light of various abuses. He singles out universal default, the practice of raising the interest rate on a particular card if the customer is delinquent paying on another (a practice he notes that American Express does not engage in). Chenault applauds initiatives by regulators (since adopted) to rein in this and other abusive practices.

In chapter 6, Nicholas Economides of New York University takes a different view of the credit card industry, arguing that its fees have been considerably higher than its costs. He attributes this situation to three factors. One is the rules the card networks impose that do not permit merchants to steer competition to cards that have the lowest fees.

Another is the requirement that merchants accept all cards issued by the networks (honor all cards). Last is that the networks set the maximum interchange fee paid by acquiring banks (those collecting on behalf of the merchants) to issuing banks (those issuing credit cards).

The honor all cards rule was recently eliminated as an outcome of an antitrust lawsuit filed by merchants against Visa and MasterCard in 2003. Interchange fees are also irrelevant now that both card networks have abolished their member ownership structure and gone public as single corporate entities. Both Visa and MasterCard, like American Express, simply assess merchants to defray the costs of operating the network. These recent developments leave Economides to argue that the first restriction—network-imposed limits on the ability of merchants to steer customers to the lowest-priced cards—likewise should be eliminated.

Thomas Brown of O'Melveny and Myers sets out in chapter 7 an alternative view of policy toward credit cards. After briefly surveying the history of payments, Brown argues that the development of the payments card is one of the more important innovations of the twentieth century—on a par with semiconductors, the cell phone, and the personal computer—yet one that consumers now take for granted. Credit cards, in particular, have fundamentally changed the way payments are made and credit is extended, by enabling consumers to tap into a line of credit without repeatedly having to go a bank loan officer to approve a loan to finance each new purchase. As other authors in this volume note, debit cards and prepaid cards are now taking an increasing share of the payments wallet, and promise change well beyond traditional point-of-sale transactions. Governments are now using prepaid cards to distribute a wide range of benefits, including unemployment insurance and workers' compensation payments, and are likely to make greater use of such cards for benefits payments in the future.

Brown recites this history to make several policy-related points. First, the federal government, by design, will always have a role in setting the policy framework for the payments industry. The U.S. Constitution gives the federal government the power to coin and regulate money.

The Federal Reserve will also continue to manage two consumer payments systems—cash and checks—even as electronic forms of payment assume greater importance.

Second, the government is essential to preserving public confidence in the integrity and reliability of all payments systems. Although technology is the first line of defense in securing electronic payments, government must be there to prosecute those who compromise that security through illegal means (such as thieves who steal consumer information from payments cards or online and use it to create counterfeit cards or transactions). At the same time, however, Brown argues that policymakers must permit financial institutions and payments networks to develop better ways of reducing fraud, without imposing liability for fraud on merchants by statute or by judicial decision. More fundamentally, government must resist the temptation to manage private payments systems, which in Brown's view runs great risks of chilling future innovation.

Conclusion

At the risk of repetition, it is clear from the chapters in this volume that consumer payments systems will continue to change, delivering ever greater benefits to users. But ultimately, as with other goods and services in the economy, payments must meet consumers' needs. There is an inherent tension between consumers' comfort with existing payments systems and the innovations in those systems that are driven by competition from payments system networks. Government policy can moderate but not eliminate this tension, by preventing fraud and other abusive practices that undermine users' trust in particular payments systems or technologies. Ultimately, however, continued advances in technology will determine how and at what cost consumers will pay for the goods and services they purchase—in ways that consumers will accept and embrace, but are unlikely to notice. Such is the fate of the financial plumbing of economies: the way money has always moved and will continue to for the foreseeable future.

Notes

1. Brian K. Bucks, Arthur B. Kennickell, Traci L. Mach, and Kevin B. Moore, "Changes in U.S. Family Finances from 2004 to 2007: Evidence from the Survey of Consumer Finances," *Federal Reserve Bulletin*, vol. 95 (February 2009), pp. A1–A56 (www.federalreserve.gov/pubs/bulletin/2009/pdf/scf09.pdf).

2. A variation of the debit card is a prepaid card, which is widely used throughout the world for urban transportation and cell phone use. Unlike debit cards, however, prepayment cards can be used only for specific purposes.

3. David S. Evans and Richard Schmalensee, *Paying with Plastic: The Digital Revolution in Buying and Borrowing*, 2nd ed. (MIT Press, 2005).

VIJAY D'SILVA

2

Payments in Flux: Megatrends Reshape the Industry

Payments is a complex industry in which change often occurs without warning. Today, three major technology trends could profoundly shift the pace and direction of evolution across the payments landscape. Industry incumbents and entrants should heed these trends to ensure their own future success.

U.S. payments evolved gradually over the last two centuries to become an industry in its own right; it is now one of the nation's largest. At approximately $280 billion in revenue, the industry now surpasses many that are better known, including airlines, hotels, television, films, and music. Competition and regulation have been important drivers of its evolution, but technology has been an especially capricious player. Frequently it changed the rules of the game in unforeseen ways, subsequently reshaping both the industry and consumer behavior. Today it again stands at the industry's gates, ready to impose significant change in diverse ways. How can institutions cope with the myriad changes that seem to arise at every turn? How do they determine which of the many strategic options are most likely to create competitive advantages? To

The author thanks Eliza Hammel, Glen Sarvady, and Tariq Shaukat of McKinsey and Company for their invaluable contributions to the development of this article.

help address such questions, I focus in this chapter on how technology is shaping the near-term evolution of the payments industry.

Surviving Landscape Upheavals

History reveals that the U.S. payments industry has seldom been quick to adopt innovation. In 1690, for example, the Massachusetts Bay Colony issued the colonies' first paper currency. Not until 1792, however, did Congress create the U.S. Mint, which produced the nation's first one-dollar coins. Throughout the first half of the nineteenth century many state-chartered banks nonetheless continued to issue their own notes. In 1862 the U.S. Treasury finally introduced America's first national paper currency, which eventually removed banks from the currency production and control processes.

Checks followed a similar pattern. Businesses and wealthy individuals used them during America's early days, but clearing was often difficult until 1914, when the Federal Reserve—created by Congress the preceding year—developed its centralized clearing system. Gradual improvements followed until the 1950s, when magnetic ink character recognition for checks was introduced, dramatically improving check-processing efficiency.

Credit cards also appeared early in the twentieth century. The concept—described as early as 1887 in Edward Bellamy's utopian novel *Looking Backward*—took root in the early 1900s when several oil companies and department stores issued credit cards to drive loyalty and improve customer service. Initially made of paper, early cards were merchant-specific and easy to replicate. It was not until 1950 that Diners Club introduced the nation's first general purpose credit card. The American Express card followed in 1958. BankAmericard, the forerunner of Visa, followed soon after. Today, 77 percent of American households use credit cards, making them one of the industry's most widespread payment instruments.

The pace of technological change quickened in the second half of the twentieth century, with adoption rates of new instruments like debit cards and electronic transactions growing faster than innovations of earlier decades. The late 1960s gave birth to ATMs; the 1970s brought automated clearinghouses that enabled banks to exchange funds electronically; the 1980s gave us data mining and advanced direct marketing approaches that enabled more aggressive card growth; and the 1990s brought these tools online with the birth of PayPal and other online payment mechanisms.

In some ways, the payments industry has become one of the most stable industries in the United States. It comprises large networks and well-established players with secure processes that enjoy significant structural and scale advantages. Still, though this industry may be slower than some to accept technological change, its pace of innovation is clearly quickening, and compelling participants to keep up.

Comprehending a Complex Industry

Payments is one of the most visible components of the financial services landscape today. Yet few people realize that it also accounts for over one-third of U.S. banking revenues, and that about three-quarters of those revenues come from consumer credit cards and transaction accounts.

Given the complexity of the industry, it is unsurprising that the payments value chain has become intricate as well. A map of payment instruments pathways between payers and payees can be useful in understanding the payments landscape. It is essential to recognize here that distinct sets of intermediaries and networks exist for paper instruments, such as cash and checks, and for nonpaper instruments, such as credit and debit cards, ACH transactions, and other instruments.

In light of the industry's varied history, its value chain has grown understandably complex, as illustrated in figure 2-1. The pathways connecting payers and payees for each type of instrument differ substantially. Each payment type has two groups of intermediaries: first, the institutions that serve the payer, such as credit card issuers and retail banks, and, second, the institutions serving the payee, such as payment

Figure 2-1. *Complexity of Payments Value Chain*

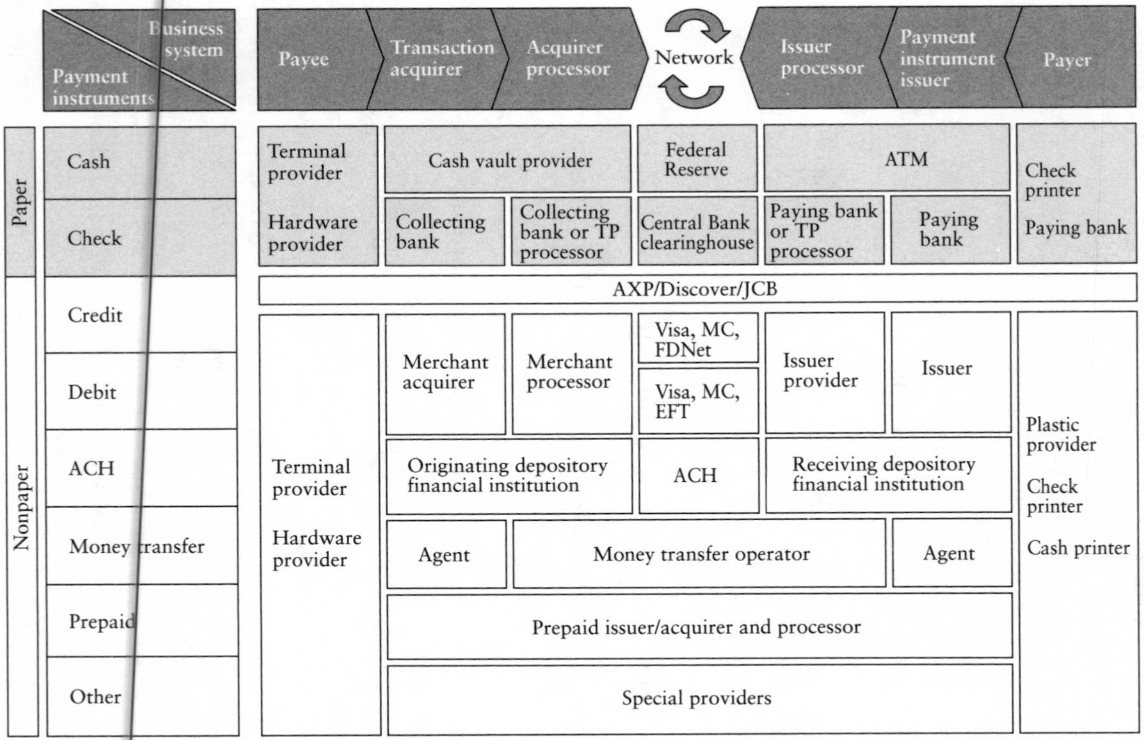

Business system / Payment instruments		Payee	Transaction acquirer	Acquirer processor	Network	Issuer processor	Payment instrument issuer	Payer
Paper	Cash	Terminal provider	Cash vault provider		Federal Reserve		ATM	
		Hardware provider						
	Check		Collecting bank	Collecting bank or TP processor	Central Bank clearinghouse	Paying bank or TP processor	Paying bank	Check printer / Paying bank
Nonpaper					AXP/Discover/JCB			
	Credit	Terminal provider	Merchant acquirer	Merchant processor	Visa, MC, FDNet	Issuer provider	Issuer	Plastic provider
	Debit				Visa, MC, EFT			Check printer
		Hardware provider						
	ACH		Originating depository financial institution		ACH	Receiving depository financial institution		Cash printer
	Money transfer		Agent	Money transfer operator			Agent	
	Prepaid			Prepaid issuer/acquirer and processor				
	Other			Special providers				

Source: McKinsey/Global Concepts.

processors and merchant acquirers for credit and debit cards. Issuers generally assume whatever credit and fraud risk is involved. Merchants typically see processors and acquirers as portals to payment systems that are vital to their business. Meanwhile, networks, including those of Visa, MasterCard, and check clearinghouses, are the backbone of the value chain. It is the parties at each end of the value chain who effectively determine which payment instruments are used and who reap the majority of the financial rewards.

Understanding the value chain diagram is important because it reveals the many steps required to process payments in today's marketplace. Many of these tasks are now automated; however, others are still labor intensive.

Although often unnoticed by consumers, technological evolution significantly affects every part of the payments value chain. Rapid advances in processing power, data storage, computer networking, wireless services, software, and business model design have clearly altered many payments operations. Underlying those changes and players' subsequent actions are three megatrends: a dramatic decline in paper check processing, a transformation of how payments networks operate, and the appearance of more sophisticated payment devices and industry entrants. These trends are fundamentally distinct and vary in visibility. Together, however, they have the ability to reconfigure the payments landscape during the coming decade.

Megatrend 1: Decline of Paper-Based Transactions

Paper-based transactions account for a significant share of transactions in most developed and developing countries. In the United States, consumers still use paper for 49 percent of payment value, of which checks account for 35 percent and cash for 14 percent (figure 2-2). By contrast, the Japanese pay only 1 percent of transactions by check and about 50 percent with cash. In emerging economies, like India's, where check payment systems are less extensively developed, cash remains the dominant payment form.

Figure 2-2. *Cash and Checks as a Share of Consumer Payments by Transaction Value, 2006*

Percent

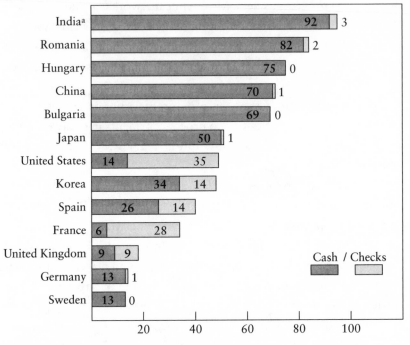

Source: McKinsey/Global Concepts, CBA, Euromonitor.
a. Check usage for India estimated at 1–3 percent, cash estimated at 91–93 percent.

Early development of a reliable and efficient check payment system partly explains why paper-based transactions in the United States remain high relative to other developed countries, such as Germany and the United Kingdom. However, two major developments threaten to change this. First, check writing in the United States has recently been declining, at about 5 percent annually overall, with even steeper declines at the point of sale (figure 2-3). Although increased card use has clearly been a factor, dramatic growth in ACH transactions is driving the trend, just as it did in some European countries. The move away from checks in the United States was initially triggered by increases in direct payroll deposits, and driven further by the proliferation of online bill paying.

Figure 2-3. *U.S. Payments Industry Volumes, by Instrument, 2007*

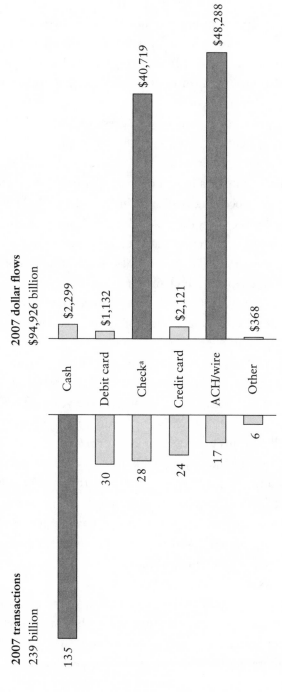

2007 transactions
239 billion

2007 dollar flows
$94,926 billion

	transactions	dollar flows
Cash	135	$2,299
Debit card	30	$1,132
Check[a]	28	$40,719
Credit card	24	$2,121
ACH/wire	17	$48,288
Other	6	$368

Source: McKinsey/Global Concepts.
a. Reflects checks paid, not checks written. Checks converted to ACH are counted in ACH.

Increasing consumer comfort with electronic payments and ongoing efforts to reduce user costs and stimulate ACH growth through online and card-based access mechanisms will fuel continuing growth until ACH becomes the dominant payment form in the United States.

The second change, that of digital check imaging, is less visible to laypeople, but also noteworthy. This is occurring faster than many anticipated: legislation passed by Congress in 2004 launched a sea change in the payments industry. The Check Clearing for the 21st Century Act—commonly referred to as Check 21—requires that banks honor digital check images in lieu of the paper originals. Enacted primarily to reduce processing costs, the impact of Check 21 is proving substantial as banks and others acquire check-imaging capabilities. Today, many banks image checks at their branches or processing facilities and others, such as USAA, have also introduced remote deposit capture—that is, enabling merchants and consumers to image checks. Some third-party providers of back-office services have also entered the game, offering check imaging services or assistance to merchants interested in developing this capability in-house.

Check imaging has already been embraced by many institutions and merchants for its potential to significantly reduce costs and spur merchant and consumer convenience. Indeed, three years after Check 21 was enacted, banks were already forwarding more than half of the nation's 23 billion transit checks in image form (figure 2-4). Checks for which the depositing and paying bank are the same are referred to as on-us checks and do not require interbank transmissions. By 2010, except for the last mile between payees and local merchants or their bank branches, we expect paper checks to have largely disappeared from the clearing process. And though banks will need to cover the fixed costs of paper-check processing for some time, eventually those and related costs will shrink by as much as two-thirds.

At the same time, the emergence of remote deposit capture introduces another risk for banks. Although today physical deposit of paper checks is an important link between merchants and their local bank branches, remote deposit capture could free merchants to shop for

Figure 2-4. *Impact of Check 21 Legislation*

Check forward presentment volume[a] (billions of items)

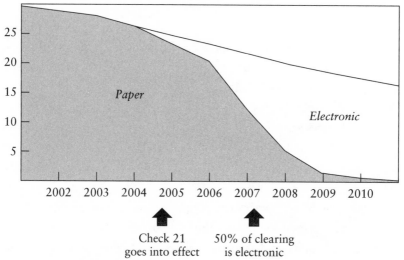

Source: McKinsey/Global Concepts.
a. Excludes on-us and ACH converted checks, includes consumers and institutions.

banking services across geographies, thereby increasing competition among banks.

Megatrend 2: Evolving Payments Networks

Check processing and ACH growth are certainly important trends, but many in the industry are rethinking what these trends could mean to the network. It helps to recognize that fundamentally there are two types of networks: closed and open. Closed systems, by definition, tend to be centralized, afford substantial security, and often use batch processing. Railroads, mainframe computers, and traditional stock exchanges are cases in point. The second type, distributed open systems, is typified by today's ubiquitous PC networks and the Internet. Open networks provide several benefits, including greater interoperability, which encourages innovation and delivers more user convenience; more resilient and less failure-prone systems; an incentive for innovation in network applications; and greater competition. Open networks, however, bring fresh concerns, including how to maintain high security levels, established operating standards, and sustainable economics.

New payment forms often begin with closed networks that address specific needs, for example, prepaid transit devices, campus meal cards, and store credit cards. By their nature, however, networks of greater size are exponentially more valuable, so developers are frequently eager to bring more transaction types under the same umbrella. For example, in the United States some fast food chains have experimented with accepting ExxonMobil's Speedpass, and in the United Kingdom, merchants in the London Underground are accepting the Oyster card, a smart card developed for transit payments.

We see five major ways in which open networks could emerge.

—Access devices could be unbundled from networks to provide improved flexibility and provide scale. Unbundling could enable the use of credit-card-like devices to access different networks (like ACH), providing a link from the point of sale to the customer's bank account. Several firms are experimenting in this arena, often motivated by increasing consumer convenience or reducing payment acceptance costs for merchants.

—Open networks could evolve through vertical growth, in which industry participants assume increasingly specialized roles across multiple instruments, usually to increase value to payees or payers. Processors, for example, might process transactions across multiple payments networks, including check, debit, and credit networks, rather than focus on a single vehicle. Or, as the relatively recent acquisitions of debit networks by Visa, MasterCard, and Discover indicate, networks themselves could consolidate to gain scale advantages.

—Large financial institutions might directly process more internal transactions where they have relationships with both the payer and payee, thus bypassing the central network altogether (on-us transactions). Notable here is the recent introduction of Pariter Solutions, a joint venture between Wells Fargo and Bank of America created to process ACH transactions between the banks and their clients. As the financial services industry consolidates, the share of on-us transactions will continue to grow.

—Networks might grow through value-added services that operate over existing networks. This could include a menu of services, such as processing, encryption, authentication, and transaction analytics. These services could increase customer loyalty from network users, and, by leveraging existing infrastructure, be quite profitable to the networks.

—Finally, there may be scenarios in which payments networks increasingly resemble the Internet with its now-common plug-and-play capabilities. In response, networks will be inclined to become more open to innovators, ultimately transforming themselves to serving less as a conduit and more as a platform provider.

Megatrend 3: Emerging Instruments and New Entrants

More visible than restructuring networks are new payment instruments that capitalize on newer technologies to make transactions more convenient for consumers and less costly for merchants. The payments industry has long been fertile ground for innovation, but the recent confluence of factors mentioned earlier is producing a groundswell of new concepts—from virtual wallets and personalized e-coupons to contactless chip cards and a host of online services. These sophisticated new instruments are finding their way into markets around the globe (figure 2-5).

Although many industry watchers track new payment instruments and predict which will succeed or fail, it is interesting to learn how such innovations arise. First, the combination of the nearly 3.5 billion mobile phones in use globally and the continuing development of mobile technology and data processing capabilities is causing phone manufacturers, network providers, and independent firms to aggressively seek opportunities to improve their foothold in the payments arena. Mobile phones are rapidly getting smarter and more multifunctional. Some firms already leverage a phone's GPS locator capability to provide tailored

Figure 2-5. New Payments Instruments, Worldwide

NOT EXHAUSTIVE

Source: Literature search; company reports.

services. Visa, for instance, is developing intelligent payments software for Google's Android phones, and telephone companies across the United States are conducting similar pilot programs.

Evidence of how technology is driving the creation of payments instruments is most apparent in Japan. NTT DOCOMO, Japan's leading phone company, introduced a mobile wallet service that spurred phenomenal growth, driven by NTT's large customer franchise. The service uses a Sony-designed microchip added to mobile phones to facilitate monetary transactions through close-proximity data transmissions. Known as Near Field Communications (NFC), this system uses a microantenna in the chip to transmit transaction data over distances of a few feet when the user waves the phone over an NFC terminal. Another mobile payments technology that gained broad acceptance is the Short Message Service

(SMS). SMS-based payments capitalize on the current popularity of text messaging, using a series of such messages between the payer and payee to complete a transaction. Like all technologies, each comes with advantages and disadvantages, and requires substantial investment to convert consumers as well as merchants. Although growth of mobile payments will likely be slow in most markets, in the long term they could emerge as a fundamental component of the payments landscape.

Next, transportation authorities are introducing faster and more efficient payment mechanisms. For instance, mass transit systems in London and Hong Kong implemented contactless payment mechanisms—the Oyster card mentioned earlier and Octopus, respectively—with much success. Across Europe, many transit and parking providers are also introducing new payment instruments, even enabling consumers to pay by their mobile phones. Given that passengers take 10.3 billion mass transit trips annually in the United States alone, the impact of further development could be substantial. In another example, many U.S. drivers are paying highway, bridge, and tunnel tolls automatically with an E-ZPass transponder that tollbooth scanners read as vehicles pass by. Many countries have similar systems in place. Collectively, speed and efficiency benefits could drive a rapid evolution of transportation-related payments over the next few years.

Another emerging area of innovation is international and national person-to-person payments. International (cross-border) remittances have recently grown at 8 percent annually to $400 billion in total flows, as advanced banking systems take root in emerging markets and immigration grows in developed markets. Formerly, remittances commonly relied on informal methods, costly transfer services, and wire transfers. In response, players like Ikobo and Xoom are working to create more efficient alternatives, and though the recent economic downturn will likely slow immigration, these opportunities should persist. Over time, domestic payments between individuals, currently at $2.9 trillion in the United States alone, could also provide substantial opportunities, particularly in online payments between individuals and small businesses.

PayPal, the large online payments subsidiary of eBay, saw its transaction volume surge past $60 billion in 2008, and is growing at about 30 percent annually.

Finally, merchants are becoming more assertive in developing or supporting parallel payments systems, often facilitated by processors. For many merchants, payments cost—particularly for credit card acceptance—is a major factor in what are often thin-margin businesses. Merchants also tend to evaluate payment instruments in terms of transaction speed and convenience, ability to drive new traffic, and impact on customer loyalty. RevolutionCard in the United States, Edy in Japan, and Squid in the United Kingdom are all attempting to bring a new value proposition to merchants; the challenge has been the reluctance of many consumers to accept yet another type of payment device.

Many of these innovations are finding rapid acceptance in outwardly different markets. In the Philippines, for instance, where the unbanked population is upwards of 75 percent, and where credit card ownership is low (0.3 cards per capita versus 3.0 in Japan), prepaid smart cards quickly achieved popularity. In Japan, Edy smart cards—named for the euro, dollar, and yen—and NTT DOCOMO's wallet-phones rapidly gained substantial market penetration.

As with innovation initiatives everywhere, however, there have also been failures. In the payments industry the long list includes Pay By Touch and Beenz. Both offered unique concepts, but had unsustainable business models. Large payments players have faced substantial risks as well. In 1996, Visa and several banks in the southern United States attempted to market a smart card during the Olympics in Atlanta, but consumer acceptance was elusive. Even government mandates intended to expedite electronic payments can fail, as Congress learned with its 1978 Electronic Funds Transfer (EFT) Act. Thirty years later Americans still write more than 30 billion checks annually.

As these three megatrends—the decline of paper processing, the transformation of payment networks, and the emergence of new devices and entrants—play out, the inevitable question becomes, what will separate the winners from the losers?

Barriers to Overcome

New payments technologies and those who strive to capitalize on them must surmount five major hurdles to succeed:

—Acceptance and critical mass. A payments network requires a virtual circle of participation with substantial numbers of both payers and payees. Innovators often underestimate the importance of rapidly building momentum and scale on both sides early on. In Japan, the market dominance of one railroad and one telephone company facilitated rapid acceptance of electronic payments instruments because they immediately appeared ubiquitous to consumers.

—Trust and authentication. Integrity is essential for success in every aspect of financial services. Credit card companies, for instance, have aggressively fought unauthorized card use for years, resulting in fraud rates that are now just a few basis points of transaction volume. But, today's rising identity theft problem highlights the critical importance of retaining trust, both in perception and reality.

—Investment process and risk. Notwithstanding some well-publicized recent missteps, financial institutions are generally risk averse, logically a desirable trait in an industry where trust is a cornerstone. But all innovation requires some risk taking, so product managers need to learn how to cope with reasonable levels of risk. Without some tolerance for failure, firms tend to move toward the sleepy, wait-and-see comfort zone, which could leave them behind.

—Organizational silos. Most banks and financial institutions, like many businesses, organize themselves by market segments or product lines. The payments industry is unique, however, bridging many of these common boundaries. Successful management therefore usually requires cross-functional teams with skills and freedoms that allow them to side-step traditional boundaries as they develop and market innovative products and services.

—Entrenched business models. Like media, pharmaceutical, and software companies, traditional payments models carry high fixed costs, such as those for technology, sales, and marketing, whereas variable costs are minimal. And like the other sectors mentioned, payments firms typically use per-unit pricing that needs to be high enough to recover fixed investment costs. Consequently, the perception of high pricing (merchant attitudes toward card fees, for example) creates an opportunity for entrants to find lower-priced alternatives for payers and payees—often by rerouting transactions over lower-priced networks. Alternatively, incumbent firms may need to change their models to protect themselves from attackers.

Each of these barriers is significant. Overcoming them will require substantial and sustained efforts that will often involve significant risk for an existing franchise.

Developing a Strategy

As the megatrends we've discussed continue to unfold and as the industry gradually acclimates to them, the balance of power could shift unpredictably, facilitating the entry of new players. These upheavals in the payments landscape will inevitably alter value chains and produce significant short-term turmoil.

As banks strategically reposition themselves to confront these trends, we believe that several guidelines will be helpful. Above all, even those with extensive knowledge and experience should avoid the dangerous polar regions of hubris and panic. And though reinforcing existing strategic advantages is sound practice, firms must also be willing to selectively cannibalize them for greater long-term gain. Focusing on customer needs by market segment should take priority over the rarely successful, one-size-fits-all approach. Financial institutions would also be wise to explore alliance, acquisition, and investment opportunities as shortcuts to participating in potentially industry-altering technologies. Deceptively simple, these steps can dramatically affect strategic outcomes and competitive positions.

For those eager to enter this complex industry, there are important cautions as well.

—Be especially cognizant of how slowly consumer payments behaviors change.

—Leverage existing infrastructure when and where possible; an established customer base is a major asset.

—Market entry requires more than marginal improvements to existing products and services; stay focused on delivering a well-differentiated user proposition.

—Recognize the substantial strength banks have in the payments business, and consider approaching them, as well as competitors, as prospective partners.

—Success in payments requires a marathon rather than a sprint mind-set.

It is difficult to predict how today's leaders of the payments industry will adapt to these trends. The changes could parallel those in the pharmaceutical industry over the last five years, where leaders shifted from developing new products internally to sourcing most of them from today's vibrant biotechnology industry. If the payments industry follows a similar path, business development and partnership activity may well skyrocket.

In the past, success in the payments industry almost demanded the creation of large stable environments built on solid foundations of trust and a highly circumspect attitude toward change. But as the pace of evolution and globalization quicken, future successes could well pivot instead on strategic flexibility and the ways institutions and companies adapt to change.

DAVID S. EVANS *and* RICHARD SCHMALENSEE

3

Innovation and Evolution of the Payments Industry

Technological developments involving the Internet, web-based software, wireless communication, computers, and data analytics are coming together in ways that promise to transform how consumers and merchants transact with each other.[1] Payments, behavioral targeting of advertising and marketing messages, location-based targeting of advertising and marketing messages, and e-commerce including mobile commerce are being integrated in ways that will transform how consumers and merchants interact with each other. Unless public policy interferes, these *mashups*[2] will likely reshape—and enhance—the payment experience for consumers and merchants.

Many commentators focus on how we will pay at the point of sale and the role that Near Field Communication (NFC) on contactless cards or mobile phones will play in that.[3] We posit that the physical method of payment—often called the form factor—will in fact vary across geography and over time as a result of past investment decisions in hardware, software, and processes in the payments ecosystem. The mashups we believe will reshape the industry as we know it today will not, however, depend on the form factor. The physical method of payment at the

We would like to thank the Brookings Institution for financial support, Karen Webster for helpful comments and suggestions, and Cheryl Morris for exceptional research support.

point of sale is a detail in a much larger transformation of the purchasing experience for consumers and merchants. To dwell only on the payment factor as enabling innovation in payments, in fact, minimizes the impact that technology will have on this industry. Our goal in this chapter is to describe how these mashups could affect the evolution of payments over the next decade.

History has shown that nothing is inevitable in the payment card industry. The cost of changing already good methods for buyers to pay sellers can well exceed the benefits of innovations. Government policy can also affect the direction of change by overruling the market and by adopting policies that, despite the best of intentions, have unanticipated adverse consequences for consumers and businesses in the complex payments industry. During this period of creative destruction now sweeping the payments industry globally, policymakers should especially heed the Hippocratic warning "Do no harm."

Electronic Payment Card Industry Today

The U.S. electronic payments industry is based on a network that moves money between consumer and merchant bank accounts using computers, software, and communication links.[4]

Origin of Payment Card Networks

The technology that underlies today's payment card networks was first widely deployed in 1979, when Visa introduced the first electronic data capturing terminal.[5] Mainframe computers did most of the processing and storage in central locations. Consumers had magnetic stripe cards and merchants had electronic terminals. At that time the merchant swiped the card through the reader to start the process of authenticating the consumer and authorizing the transaction. The swipe initiated a signal that traveled through a series of intermediate computers that switched the transaction to a central processing unit. By exchanging signals with the cardholder's bank to assess the cardholder's account, this unit then determined whether to authorize the transaction. If the transaction was authorized, the unit then exchanged signals with other computers on the network to move the designated amount from the cardholder's bank to the merchant's bank. The various computers were connected over private networks that interconnected as necessary.

One can think of this computer system as being based on the interaction of two thin clients[6] at the point of sale: the magnetic stripe card that contained a small amount of data on the consumer, and the point-of-sale device that contained little intelligence. Most of the work for the network was done at various hubs, especially the central one belonging to the owner of the card scheme, which consisted of multiple large computers. MasterCard and Visa have upgraded their systems over time but the basic architecture has remained the same.

These networks are more complicated than they might seem at first glance. At the periphery of the networks are individual merchants, the larger of which operate in many locations. These merchants have installed various software and hardware for accepting cards over time. More than forty-five vendors supply the point-of-sale equipment and nearly 1,000 software systems on the market are incorporated into the point-of-sale equipment.[7]

The merchants on the network typically have a relationship with an acquiring bank and a merchant processor, which in turn operates remote computer-based platforms that perform a variety of steps between the merchant and the card system. There are nine major processors in the United States. The larger ones operate several different platforms. Chase Paymentech has two major platforms, for example, and First Data Corporation has between four and ten processing platforms depending on payment type.[8]

Over time, every application vendor has developed its software to work with the other essential parts of the overall network. But the modern payment card industry is much like a large corporation that, through mergers and changes in vendors over time, has numerous computer systems and software packages jury-rigged together. Much of the software is based on older languages rather than what is being used to build modern web-based businesses.

This fragmented structure imposes significant practical constraints on innovation. It is difficult to make a change at any point in the network if that change is incompatible with hardware or software used at other points. An innovator would have to convince other network participants to make compatible changes. These changes may require significant investments. The innovator must either absorb these costs or persuade other participants that it is worth incurring them without necessarily knowing that other participants will. As a result, innovation can be slow and may be biased toward improvements that are compatible with the existing infrastructure. In the next section, we discuss how this disjointed structure impedes collecting and analyzing data from merchants and consumers. But, as we also discuss, this infrastructure has fueled much of the innovation emerging as entrepreneurs begin to use new computing technologies that essentially work around these constraints.

Technological Progress in the Face of Inertia

Despite this seemingly archaic structure, and the legacy hardware and software beneath it, the payment card system has experienced great technological progress in the last three decades and works extremely well. The average time it takes a consumer and merchant to complete a card transaction has declined dramatically (as anyone older than forty is well aware). Although the time varies depending on the point-of-sale equipment the merchant uses, the average time for completing a credit card transaction is now approximately seventeen seconds, versus seventy-three seconds for checks.[9]

This technological progress has resulted in part from the broader revolution in computers and communications. Improvements in computer speed and capacity have more than kept pace with the increase in the volume of transactions. Telecommunications have become cheaper and more reliable. Point-of-sale equipment has benefited from the miniaturization of computers. Improvements in computing capacity and software have enabled better and faster risk management.

Most important, consumers are generally happy with the payment experience at the point of sale. In a recent survey, we asked 550 consumers to rank the importance of various aspects of their payment experience in physical stores.[10] The results revealed that most consumers are generally content with their current payment experience and showed little interest in changing their current use of magnetic swipe cards to contactless cards, mobile phones, or other emerging technologies.[11] What they want is security, convenience, ease of use, and available flexible financing options.[12]

We have not performed a survey of merchants, but have seen no evidence that they are dissatisfied with the mechanics of accepting payment by cards at their points of sale. Thus far the vast majority of merchants have not embraced any of the various alternative methods of payment that have been introduced in the last several years, such as contactless.[13] They, of course, would like to pay lower merchant fees when a consumer does pay with plastic.[14] The payment card system is based on technology that is several generations old. To understand why this system nevertheless forms the basis for the mashups that we believe will reshape the payments industry, it is useful to digress on the evolution of modern computer systems.

Modern Computer Systems

Until recently, computer networks connected client computers over private local area networks or private wide area networks to server computers that provided these clients with access to centralized resources. For example, a spreadsheet developed on a local computer using a local software application quite possibly accessed data stored on a server computer and was sent to colleagues by e-mail through another server computer. The payment card system is one large private network based on mainframe computers, servers, and proprietary software running on many interconnected systems.

With the rise of the Internet, this model has begun shifting to what is known as *cloud computing*, in which much of the processing and storage takes place on server computers owned by a third party and accessed over the Internet. Many widely used applications—such as Facebook, Google Calendar, MSN Instant Messenger, iTunes, and Salesforce.com—

are "in the cloud." Many of the interesting innovations in payments will likely take place in the cloud rather than on private networks.

As computation has moved from the desktop to servers on private networks to servers in the cloud, clients can become thinner—at least in terms of the fraction of the overall workload they perform. Moreover, over time computer networks have become more interoperable. The standardization of the industry on the Wintel platform during the late 1980s and 1990s made it easier to interchange software and hardware than in the fragmented world of multiple platforms that preceded it. The development of HTML, HTTP, and other Internet protocols has provided a standard platform for web-based and cloud-based computing. It has also made the standardization of desktop software and hardware less important, because Internet standards define an interface between the cloud and the desktop that can be used by any standards-compliant browser running on any operating system.

Yet, as thin as clients could be in the cloud-based world, nothing is as slim—or as dumb—as the magnetic stripe card, which uses a technology that one might have thought would have been phased out alongside cassette tapes. There has, however, always been great inertia in the payments industry because change requires a vast multitude of buyers and sellers to modify their behavior and make new investments. The magnetic stripe card itself became the standard in the payment card industry in part because MasterCard and Visa subsidized, through reduced interchange fees, initial adoption of electronic terminals at the point of sale.

Possibilities for Change

Indeed, cash has remained the most popular form of payments worldwide because of its tremendous convenience and simplicity.[15] The widespread availability of cash-dispensing machines that the consumer accesses with a card has even given cash a new lease on life. In the United States, it has also proved difficult to wean consumers and businesses away from checks. Despite the proliferation of new methods of paying bills online, many households continue to write paper checks. A recent survey of small businesses found that these entities prefer to send out paper invoices and receive payments by check.[16] Such inertia applies to cards themselves. The magnetic stripe card is the preferred form factor for credit and debit card transactions in many countries, including the United States. A recent survey found that, after more than three years of effort to put contactless cards in the hands of consumers and to persuade merchants to install contactless terminals at the point of sale, 83 percent of American consumers had still not used contactless and only 1 percent of store locations accepting credit cards had installed the necessary technology to accept these cards.[17]

Although change in the payments industry may seem glacial, even glaciers can make substantial progress over time. The most important trend is the movement to digital money, in which a computing device captures the transaction. The share of payments that are electronic has steadily increased over time. Figure 3-1 shows estimates of the share of various electronic payments methods over time for the United States.

As of 2007 in the United States, electronic payments accounted for two-thirds of all noncash payments by number and 45 percent by value.[18] When payments involve the transmission of bits, it becomes easier to integrate the payments aspect of a transaction into many other complementary services and to create synergies among these various services. It does not matter whether the payment is captured by a computer in the cloud using a not-very-smart magnetic stripe card as the authentication device or a browser-based mobile phone. As long as the transaction is digital, numerous mashup possibilities reveal themselves. Moreover, the development of these complementary services (which are based on digital transactions) will increase the value of digital relative to nondigital forms of payment and thereby accelerate the adoption of digital forms of payment. Thus, though paper-based payments will no doubt persist for the foreseeable future, even in developed economies, a revolution in the transaction experience—that is, all the services that relate to buyers and sellers getting together—will likely lead to a rapid increase in the rate of adoption of digital forms of payment.

Figure 3-1. *Estimated Total Number of Transactions,*
by Payment Type

Number of transactions (billions)

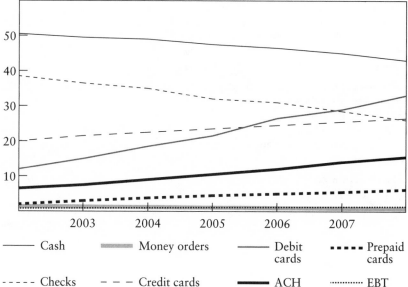

Cash Money orders Debit cards Prepaid cards

Checks Credit cards ACH EBT

Source: Nilson Report, Federal Reserve, NACHA, *ATM&Debit News*; authors' calculations.

Before describing the mashups this will likely involve, we explore some economic aspects of the adoption of new technologies and business models in the payments industry.

Technology in the Payments Industry

Anyone talking about revolutionary change in the payments industry—especially when it comes to how we pay—should be greeted with significant skepticism. Cash has remained the main form of payment ever since metallic money was introduced in 700 BC. Every few years someone predicts its imminent demise.

People have been paying with magnetic stripe cards only since the early 1980s, yet pundits predict its imminent replacement by contactless

Table 3-1. *Recent Analyst Forecasts of Adoption of Alternative Payment Form Factors*

Contactless credit and debit card payments (sometimes called proximity payments), mobile payments (m-payments), and biometrically authenticated payments will each levy its own unique impact over the next five years. Together, they could garner over $400 billion in revenue by 2011.	The Pelorus Group 2006
57 million consumers will be using chip-embedded credit cards to make contactless payments by 2013, which is more than double the 24.8 million in 2008 and will be bolstered primarily by expansion of contactless products into gift cards and private label cards.	The Javelin Group 2008
The gross transaction value of mobile payments will exceed $300 billion internationally by 2013.	Juniper Research 2008
As many as 612 million mobile users will generate transactions on the order of US$587 billion during 2011 by their phones.	Jupiter Research 2008

Source: Authors' tabulations.

chip devices that users can wave at the point of sale, various mobile phone solutions, and the odd assortment of biometric methods including the fingerprint.[19] Table 3-1 presents a few of the predictions. However, just as cash has endured, so has the technologically unhip mag-stripe card—the form factor of choice for most of the world's credit and debit account users.

The apparent resistance of the payments industry to innovation seems to stem from a basic economic characteristic of all payments systems.

The Chicken and Egg Problem for Two-Sided Platforms

The payments industry creates value by providing a method that both buyers and sellers use to consummate transactions. The insight of the ancient inventors of standard gold coins was that trade would be much easier if there were a generally accepted and uniform method of payment. Fixing prices in standard gold coins was easier than using irregular lumps of metal or oxen or roosters. The invention of the general purpose payment card was hardly as profound. But in many circumstances cards with deferred billing and payment agreements enabled consumers and merchants to engage in transactions that could not occur otherwise, given that the consumer did not carry or did not want to carry large amounts of cash.

To create a standard of payment requires, however, that buyers and sellers agree to accept it and use it. Buyers will not use a payments instrument if they cannot pay with it where they shop, and sellers will not go to the trouble of accepting one if few shoppers want to pay with it. Entrepreneurs looking to introduce a new way of paying must solve this fundamental chicken and egg problem. Doing so has become more difficult over time because these entrepreneurs compete against increasingly secure and convenient payment methods through which transactions take only a few seconds to complete. It is hard to convince merchants and consumers to change when what they currently rely on works very well.

The payments industry is based on what economists call a two-sided platform[20]—a business that creates value by inducing two groups of customers to come together, each of whose members obtain value by interacting with members of the other group. Shopping malls, financial exchanges, auction markets, multiple listing services, advertising-supported media, software platforms, and video game consoles are all examples. In all these cases, a participant on one side gets more value from being part of a platform with more participants on the other side. Video game console users get more value from consoles that have more games, and game developers get more value from consoles that have more users. For many two-sided platforms—and this is particularly true of payments—it is very difficult to get users on one side unless there are users on the other side. The chickens and eggs have to appear almost simultaneously.

Basic Economics of Consumer and Merchant Adoption

Merchants consider up-front and variable costs of using a payment method. The up-front costs include training sales staff in how to handle the payment, modifying accounting systems, and—especially with solutions that involve authentication at the point of sale such as payment cards—equipment and possibly integration with their information technology systems. Variable costs include merchant fees for cards or cash and check handling costs, as well as changes in the numbers of checkout lanes and clerks needed to process transactions. If that were the end of the story, merchants would only adopt a new payments system if it were cheaper[21] and if enough consumers switched their transactions to it to warrant the investment in up-front costs.

But cost is not all that matters. Accepting a new payment method at a store may also result in customers shopping there who would not have done so otherwise. Likewise, accepting a new payment method may convince customers to buy more as a result of using that method. Shoppers may like a payment method more because it is more convenient or secure for them or because they are getting some sort of reward for using it. Having more shoppers (and more shopping) results in incremental sales. The merchant makes a profit margin on these sales, and so accepting a new payment method may in fact lead to incremental margins.

The key insight about the acceptance of new payment methods is that incremental margins are often a more significant economic factor in merchant decisions than saving money on merchant fees and other ongoing transaction costs. The profit margin on additional sales averages 29 percent for large merchants. The average cost of accepting a payment method is in the range of 1 to 2 percent of the transaction size.[22]

Consider two payment alternatives for a merchant with $100 million of annual transactions. One promises a 50 percent reduction in payment costs—1 percent—for 20 percent of transactions that would take place using that method. That leads to a cost savings of .01 x $20 million or $200,000. The other promises a 3 percent increase in overall sales as a result of attracting new shoppers. That increases sales by $3 million and leads to increased profits of $870,000 on average. In fact, it would only take a .7 percent increase in sales to beat the method that offers a 50 percent reduction in payment costs.

A card system that can build up a significant number of users therefore has a very compelling proposition to merchants, for which it can charge a significant merchant fee. Consider a card that 10 percent of shoppers would use for transactions and assume that 70 percent of their transactions displace other transactions but that the remaining 30 percent are incremental. In the earlier example, the increase in incremental margin is $870,000. The merchant would therefore be willing to pay, roughly, up to $870,000 of additional transaction fees on the 70 percent of overall transactions that are displaced. That works out to a transaction fee of 12.4 percent $(870,000/(0.1*0.7*100 \text{ million}) = .124)$.

Of course, consumers will not take a card if they cannot use it. They must believe that they will be able to use it at a wide range of merchants to pay. That gives rise to the chicken and egg problem. Diners Club resolved it in 1950 by signing up a few restaurants that would be of interest to its Manhattan account holders and a few account holders who would be of interest to those restaurants. There was apparently enough value for both sides to get on board initially. The restaurants just had to keep track of a few receipts, and the account holders did not yet have a wallet full of competing cards. American Express resolved the problem by buying merchant and cardholder accounts from other small systems. MasterCard and Visa, as cooperatives, did so by having individual banks sign up merchants and cardholders in several local areas.

Consider the introduction of the Discover Card by Sears in 1986, one of the greatest business success stories in a decade of success stories. In its first year, Sears persuaded more than 11 million of the 25 million Sears store cardholders to sign up for a Discover Card that would enable them to pay at a variety of merchants and convinced some 500,000 merchant locations to accept the card.[23] Merchants had good reason to believe that millions of consumers would be carrying the Discover Card, given that Sears already had access to 25 million Sears cardholders and was offering its Discover cardholders 5 percent cash back on purchases. Accordingly, enough merchant locations accepted the card in its first year to make it valuable to the cardholders.

Economics and experience point to a critical lesson. It is very difficult to persuade merchants to adopt a new payment alternative unless enough consumers value the alternative so much that they will not shop at that merchant or will buy less unless the merchant offers that alternative. The prospect of incremental sales can provide enough value to pull merchants into accepting a new method. Shaving the already small transaction fees by switching consumers to a cheaper payment alternative generally cannot. Many new payment alternatives in recent years have bought into the fool's gold of merchants clamoring for cheaper payment alternatives. Merchants would, of course, like their existing payment alternatives to be cheaper, but they will not eagerly incur upfront costs and change processes just for slightly lower merchant fees.

The Role of Inertia

As the payment card system has developed over the last half century, considerable investments have gone into developing networks that connect millions of merchants around the globe to hundreds of millions of cardholders. Merchants, merchant processors, merchant acquirers, card networks, card processors, issuers, and many other suppliers to these entities have invested in hardware and software for handling payments. They have also invested in internal processes that result in human capital investments. This legacy leads to inertia for two reasons.

The first is that many participants in the payment ecosystem have made sunk investments in equipment, software, and people. In many cases these investments have been largely depreciated. New technology is therefore competing with old technology that has little, if any, ongoing cost. The second reason is that many of these investments are interdependent, as mentioned earlier. It may not be possible to change the point-of-sale technology without also changing the point-of-sale software and the merchant processing platforms. It may not be possible to change the merchant processing platforms without changing point-of-sale technology or the network software.

The investments made in payment systems also lead to what is called *path dependence*. The value of adopting new technology at a given time depends on the history of previous investments. A country that has made no investments can choose the best of new technology based on the net benefits of available alternative technologies. A country that has made significant past investments will have to factor in the cost of changing its infrastructure and the fact that the marginal cost of its old technology may be very low. Many countries—from China to Mexico—with low penetration of point-of-sale equipment and other investments in payment systems face very different economic decisions concerning adopting new technology than those countries with high levels of penetration and investment.

The consumer also has some inertia. People have gotten used to using cards in a particular way at the checkout. It usually works quite well: people sign or enter a PIN and either way the transaction takes place in a matter of seconds. Any change—any innovation—has to overcome this inertia. It must provide enough value to merchants and consumers alike so that both have an incentive to try something new.

Dealing with Inertia

Several new card innovations that have been introduced in the last few years illustrate the practical impact of inertia in payments.

Pay By Touch was founded in 2002 as a new system based on fingerprint authentication. The consumer registered her fingerprint at a kiosk and assigned her fingerprint to a particular payment method. Pay By Touch encouraged consumers to associate their fingerprint with their checking account just as PayPal encourages its account holders to use their checking accounts. This eliminated the merchant fees from the card systems and enabled Pay By Touch to offer merchants a potentially cheaper way of paying for transactions.

To use Pay By Touch consumers had to accept registering and paying with their fingerprints. Merchants had to install point-of-sale equipment that authenticated payments with fingerprints and to switch transactions to the Pay By Touch system. Pay By Touch also needed at least some merchants to install kiosks where consumers could register their fingerprints.

Pay By Touch raised more than $300 million in capital. Targeting independently owned grocers, between its launch and 2007 it persuaded only one significant such merchant to accept the new payment method—PigglyWiggly, a chain of 600 independently owned stores primarily in small to midsized towns in the Midwest and South.[24] Pay By Touch filed for bankruptcy on December 14, 2007, and closed its system down shortly thereafter.[25] Although the firm faced many problems, including squabbles among its partners, the fact remains that it obtained little merchant or consumer participation and no one has further pursued its proposed model.

The problem Pay By Touch faced is obvious in retrospect: it required merchants to make significant investments in point-of-sale technology. These investments would make sense only if enough consumers started paying with their fingers (associated with a checking account) rather than with a card so that merchants could save on card fees, or if enough consumers decided they would transact only if they could pay with their fingers so that merchants would capture incremental sales. Pay By Touch, however, did not have a compelling enough proposition for the consumer. The consumer had to go to the trouble of registering her fingerprint. Because she could then pay with her finger only at a limited number of locations, she still had to carry cards. It is unclear how much time the consumer saved at checkout when she paid with her finger. Pay By Touch counted on the novelty of paying with the finger to convince consumers to come on board their platform, but it was not enough.

The Octopus card is a contactless prepaid payment method in wide use in Hong Kong. It was initially sponsored by the Hong Kong subway as a convenient way for customers to pay and as a way for the subway to reduce queues and save on resources. In 1997, in the first three months of its entrance into the market, more than 3 million cards were in consumers' hands. Today, with 17 million Octopus cards in circulation, more than 95 percent of Hong Kong residents between the ages of sixteen and sixty-five carry the card.[26] With this base Octopus has been able to persuade merchants to accept the card for payment, a particularly attractive proposition to merchants in the malls at the subway stations.

Since 2000, when the card was first offered to merchants, 16,000 retail outlets have agreed to accept it and many have also installed equipment for consumers to load the card with money.[27] Octopus has expanded its contactless payment devices to include many other form factors with contactless chips, including watches.[28] The key to Octopus's success was having that critical mass of account holders through its initial alliance with the subway system.

The experience with contactless systems in the United States has been quite different. MasterCard and Visa introduced contactless cards in 2003 and 2005 respectively. Over the next several years MasterCard and Visa issuing banks distributed 35 million contactless cards, most of which were replacements of cards for existing account holders. These cards also had magnetic stripes and therefore could be used in the usual way, as well as by waving at a contactless reader at merchants that had these readers. MasterCard and Visa persuaded a few large national chains to install contactless readers, including McDonald's, 7-Eleven, Walgreens, and CVS. The rate of installation of contactless readers at the point of sale, however, has gone much more slowly than was anticipated.[29] Of approximately 6 million merchant locations in the United States, only 40,000—fewer than 1 percent—have contactless readers installed, with most concentrated in multistate quick service restaurants and convenience stores.[30]

Merchants have not installed contactless readers because they do not see the economic benefit. The cards do not lead to significant cost savings at most merchants because they incur the same merchant fees as regular credit and debit cards, and the cost savings from increased transaction speed is modest compared to the cost of changing point-of-sale technology. The main benefit to merchants would therefore be margins from incremental sales. But to make an investment in more expensive point-of-sale technology merchants need to be persuaded that enough consumers would adopt contactless cards and that enough of those cardholders would refuse to shop at a merchant that did not accept the cards. However, there is not a strong interest on the part of consumers, even though millions have the cards in their wallets. Consumers save time mainly in situations where they can wave the card and not sign a receipt. The card systems, though, require signatures for transactions over $25 (sometimes increased to $50 by the merchant), which means that consumers save little time for many of the transactions where they normally use cards. In the United States, predictions of contactless penetration have fallen steadily with experience. Five years after the introduction of contactless by MasterCard, 91 percent of cardholders, based on a recent survey, never used it.[31]

BillMeLater is a successful entrant into the payments business in the United States. Consumers who click on the BillMeLater alternative at the checkout for an online retailer are prompted for the last four digits of their social security number and date of birth. If the consumer is approved after a credit-risk analysis, BillMeLater pays the e-tailer and bills the consumer later. BillMeLater often provides promotional financing, such as to pay in ninety days or to pay in installments, in concert with the e-tailer. Consumers who choose to do so become BillMeLater account holders and, depending on their payment history, will be approved for larger amounts in subsequent transactions.

To begin operations, BillMeLater had to persuade a merchant that if it offered BillMeLater on its website enough consumers would use it to drive incremental sales to those merchants. Consumers did not have to have existing accounts; they just needed to be attracted to the convenience of the BillMeLater payment alternative and the finance offer. The chicken and egg problem was therefore less serious than it would have been had consumers had to go through the tedious process of applying for a card and carrying it around, or had merchants had to incur significant costs for upgrading their hardware and software. Since starting in 2001 BillMeLater has, as of August 2008, more than 450 online retailers that accept its payment method and more than 4 million accountholders.[32]

Much of the discussion about payment card alternatives has focused on methods that provide services to merchants and cardholders that are similar to those offered by traditional payment card systems but come at a lower cost to the merchant. Some discussion has focused on some form factor innovation that is appealing to consumers. The leading alternative payment methods for the physical point of sale introduced in the United States in the last several years include Tempo, Revolution Money, and Pay by Touch. Their business models all entailed offering lower merchant fees than traditional card systems offered. Other technological changes, such as contactless and various methods of using the mobile phone to make payments, offer a somewhat different way of paying. These have largely failed because they do not offer consumers enough additional convenience or value to modify how they have been paying at the point of sale for many years.[33]

We believe that the real revolution in the payments industry is not going to come from improving the basic payment transaction between consumers and merchants. There is simply not much room for making transaction processing faster or cheaper and therefore relatively few benefits accrue to consumers or merchants. Instead, the revolution will come from the mashup of payments with technologies and business models outside the traditional payment card industry. Those have the potential to provide significant additional value to consumers and merchants above and beyond efficient transaction processing. The form factor is relevant for these mashups only insofar as it can facilitate their occurrence.

Monetizing Transaction Data

In the United States alone, millions of transactions flow through the electronic payment systems each day. In the course of authenticating the cardholder, authorizing the transaction, and settling the charges, the various players in the payment card ecosystem collect a great deal of data. Data are captured on who the consumer is, what her socioeconomic background is, what merchant she shopped at, how much she spent, and even potentially what she bought, given that many merchants collect SKU-level data on purchases.[34]

It goes too far to say that these data are flushed down the drain. But to the extent they are used, it is only in primitive ways, such as for cross-promotional activities with merchants and for merchant loyalty programs. The online advertising industry has revealed, however, that these data have immense value. Not surprisingly, many firms in and outside the electronic payment card industry are exploring ways to use these data.

We begin by describing how the online advertising industry uses data collected from what users do online today and then explain how transaction data could be used to add more value to consumers and merchants.

The Online Advertising Industry

The online advertising industry accounted for 14 percent of advertising spending in the United States in 2007 and is predicted to grow to about 17.4 percent in 2008. In part advertisers are following the audience. Search and display advertising is the most revolutionary aspect of online advertising and together accounted for 72 percent of online advertising spending in 2007—the remainder went to e-mail advertising and classified listings.[35]

The companies that provide search engines sell advertisers space on the pages that display the search results. The user who clicks on the ad is taken to the advertiser's website, where the advertiser will typically try to sell the searcher something. Advertisers can bid on placing ads on the search results pages for particular keywords or combinations of keywords. Advertisers pay a cost-per-click (CPC) when a consumer clicks their ad. Roughly speaking, companies auction off slots on the search-results pages based on how much in total advertisers are willing to pay for the slot. This depends on the CPC and the number of clicks they draw in.

Advertising also appears on web pages that attract viewers with content other than search results. This could be content that is provided by portals such as Yahoo!, publisher sites like CNN.com, and social networking sites such as Facebook. These display ads, as they are called, look similar to those in newspapers and magazines. Several slots on the page are devoted to ads that contain text, pictures, or video. Unlike traditional advertisements, however, when viewers point and click they are taken to a web page just as they are when they complete a search. Nevertheless, like traditional advertisements, advertisers pay for display ads based on the cost-per-thousand (CPM) viewers where the CPM is adjusted based on the demographic characteristics of the audience. These ads are sold just like traditional advertisements.

Online advertising is not just a PC phenomenon. Many other devices are now connected to the Internet and therefore are capable of delivering online advertising. These include mobile phones, which many argue will be a larger source of online advertising than PCs, and eventually video game consoles, televisions, and other handheld devices.[36]

Online advertising can provide much more measurable and relevant marketing than traditional advertising can. First, consumers reveal something about themselves when they search on a set of keywords ("thin crust pizza Boston") or visit a particular website (one that offers reviews of laptop computers). Computers can, and do, display advertisements tailored to the visitors and are therefore likely to be far more relevant than what visitors would see in traditional media. Second, the IP address of the person looking at a web page at a particular time, coupled with a variety of other data that can be associated with that IP address, can provide a great deal of information—for example, that the visitor lives in New Canaan, Connecticut, has recently looked for baby clothes online, and was browsing at eleven o'clock in the morning on a weekday.

The online advertisements are also more actionable because they are typically links to a product or service. When viewers click the ad—which almost all web users now know they can and are meant to do—they are redirected to a site chosen by the advertiser. The site could provide more information or enable the viewer to make a purchase. Whether the viewer is driven by the desire for instant gratification or the convenience of finding and buying things online, the advertiser is happy to achieve its ultimate objective: to make a sale or, as it is sometimes known, a conversion.

An important development in online advertising now concerns behavioral targeting. By collecting and processing more data on consumers, sellers of advertising could target advertising more precisely, potentially in real time. Such targeting could enable these sellers to provide consumers and advertisers with much more relevant, and hence mutually valuable, advertisements. On the other hand, this sort of targeting has raised significant concerns over privacy that may drive public policy in directions that would retard or even prevent value-creating innovation.

We hope that public policy reflects the fact that this revolution in advertising, if it is allowed to occur, will leave both consumers and merchants better off. Consumers will receive more relevant ads and have to endure far fewer about products and services they do not care about. Targeted advertising enables better use of consumers' time and provides them with more valuable information. Advertisers provide information more efficiently to consumers who value it and who are therefore more likely to buy their goods or services. Technological advances that can provide more relevant and actionable ads for merchants and consumers will provide tremendous benefits to the economy.

Despite its clear technological advantages over traditional advertising today, the online advertising industry still relies on brute force in targeting viewers. Most computer users have on their systems countless cookies—information nuggets that track visits to websites—inserted by various players in the online advertising business. In addition, search engines record and store the search history of each user. Google even scans the e-mail of its Gmail customers. Many of these data can be correlated with those in other databases tied to the same user or IP address. If combined, entities in the online advertising business could have at their disposal rich detail on the vast majority of Internet users. Great effort is being invested in the development of behavioral targeting, which tries to glean, in addition to their personal characteristics, from these sorts of data what is on people's minds in terms of shopping.[37] Most online advertising today, however, does not use much of this information. Display ads are more typically based almost entirely on location, time of day, and some knowledge of the profile of the typical visitor to a particular site.

There are two challenges to the development of sophisticated methods for targeting. One, already mentioned, concerns privacy. The use of private information has generated some backlash from privacy advocacy groups, the government, and various user groups.[38] Facebook was heavily criticized for its launch of the Beacon advertisement system in November 2007 that pushed data from third-party sites (you just bought some concert tickets) to someone's Facebook friends (all of your friends see an update that you bought those tickets). Part of the backlash has resulted because participants in the online advertising industry have tracked and retained data on users without their knowledge and consent.[39] There is now a race between self-regulation and government regulation of the use of data. In the last year Google, under intense pressure from European regulators, moved from keeping search data forever, to keeping it for eighteen months, to keeping it "just" nine months.

The other challenge is technological. Most online advertising is delivered in what appears to be real time. When a visitor goes to a web page, the advertising looks as though it is an integral part of that page, just like the page of a magazine would look. In fact, when a visitor clicks on that page, various server computers in the online advertising business are making quick decisions on what ad to show next. It all happens so quickly that the human eye is incapable of noticing. An important problem with behavioral targeting and other sophisticated methods for using data is that they require vast amounts of computation to be performed in nanoseconds if advertising is to be delivered without viewers noticing any delay.

Economic Value of Consumer Preference Data

The information used for online advertising is a weak sister of what is available through the electronic payments industry. Take the earlier example of the person whose IP address was identified as being in New Canaan. Online advertising infers that the person is a young mother because the website she visited sells baby clothes, that she is not at work because she was surfing at eleven o'clock in the morning, and that she is well off financially because her IP address correlates to New Canaan. The visitor, however, could have been the housekeeper, a grandmother or aunt, or a friend who wants to buy a present for a new baby. The individual may or may not be well off because not everyone in New Canaan is. Suppose that online advertisers had access to the person's credit card purchasing history. The amount spent, where the person has shopped, and possibly what the person has bought would be highly relevant information on this individual. Moreover, the credit card purchasing history is factual, whereas online advertisers can often make only educated guesses.

Consider another aspect of online advertising. Advertisers would like to know how effective their advertisements have been. Have viewers purchased the advertiser's product after viewing an ad? Online advertisers often know (through cookies or other tracking methods) whether an individual who saw a display ad for a new electronic device went to the advertiser's online store to purchase it. But because most goods continue to be sold in physical stores—and probably will continue to be—there is no convenient way to track what happens once a person leaves the Internet. Maybe our Internet user in New Canaan saw a promotion for CVS when the store was offering a sale on Pampers. The credit or debit card transaction would indicate definitively that the individual actually went to CVS and could in the future also confirm that the user not only purchased Pampers but purchased a particular size.

This level of information is obviously quite valuable for both the consumer and the advertiser. Once the online advertising industry knows that the individual is a well-off young mother with a newborn baby, it can present her with ads tailored to her likely needs. With the online advertising industry acting as an intermediary, advertisers such as Procter & Gamble can target their advertising to this woman. Instead of wasting her time with products more suitable for men or older women, she will see ads relevant to her. Moreover, Procter & Gamble will value the fact that it can determine how effective its advertising has been. Advertisers can examine whether the people who actually viewed their ads actually went out and bought their products; with very aggregate data on viewership and sales, they can only approximate that now.

The payment transaction data could be mashed up in three ways. They could be used to better target traditional display and search ads and assess the effectiveness of these ads. We surmise that Google Checkout will be used this way although Google has not formally disclosed its intent. The data could be used to enhance existing direct marketing efforts such as sending individuals a coupon that could be used to purchase the good or offer a rebate directly to a particular payment card. American Express and others have done this by mailing promotions to cardholders in concert with merchants. New online advertising technologies could sharpen this focus. Cardlytics is developing an advertising network for financial institutions following these principles. It is developing technology for helping financial institutions display advertising and other marketing messages on online banking pages and on credit card portals for bill payment. The data could also be used as part of a location-based promotions drive, during which consumers receive an advertising message on their mobile phones when they are near a store, depending, perhaps, on their past purchases. Such location-based methods promise to be the most transforming because they can truly drive incremental sales to merchants. Cellfire has pioneered many aspects of mobile couponing and location-based promotions.[40]

In all three cases, we may see payments and online advertising business models start to mash up, and the technologies developed for online advertising used to target marketing and advertising using transaction data. New businesses might be behind these combinations—some may act as intermediaries between the online advertising and payments industries. Existing businesses might extend themselves. A financial institution, for example, might consider using payments data to provide advertising and marketing that help their payments business and cross-sell other products, driving additional revenue. Businesses from these two ecosystems—Yahoo! and MasterCard, for example—might themselves be mashed up through a merger or acquisition. They are both, after all, businesses built on the manipulation of data over networks.

The mobile phone has the potential to play a central role in this integration of transaction data and advertising.

Mobile Phone Revolution

The mobile telephone has become the world's most ubiquitous technology. There are more than 3.5 billion mobile telephones in use today globally, nearly four times the number of PCs and two times the number of television sets.[41] Table 3-2 shows mobile phone subscriber penetration as a fraction of total population for various countries. The growth of mobile phones in the emerging and lesser developed countries is an example of the path dependence observation we made previously. Countries that had made little investment in fixed-line telephone systems simply leapfrogged the old technology and went with the new. In many parts of the world there have already been mashups of mobile phones and payments that have responded to particular local circumstances. Only a portion of the potential synergies between the mobile handset, mobile communications, and payments have yet been realized.

Development of Mobile Technology

Mobile phone technology is evolving rapidly. Although a large portion of the stock of mobile phones around the world consists of "dumb" devices, people replace their mobile phones relatively frequently. Much of the stock of mobile phones in five years is likely to consist of devices that are powerful computers, run by sophisticated software platforms, with many applications available. Many of these phones are likely to be connected to the Internet and have browsers.[42]

Three aspects of mobile phone technology can prove important for mashups with payments.

—Internet connectivity. An increasing portion of mobile phones have browsers and can be linked to the Internet. As of May 2008, 95 million mobile subscribers (37 percent of all subscribers) in the United States paid for mobile access to the Internet. As more recent numbers are published, this penetration will likely increase with the entry of devices that

Table 3-2. *Mobile Phone Penetration for Various Countries*[a]

Country	Penetration	Country	Penetration	Country	Penetration
Worldwide	47	Guatemala	76	Philippines	51
Argentina	102	Hong Kong	146	Poland	109
Australia	102	Hungary	110	Portugal	126
Austria	117	Iceland	115	Qatar	150
Bolivia	34	India	20	Romania	107
Brazil	63	Indonesia	35	Russia	119
Bulgaria	130	Iran	42	Saudi Arabia	115
Canada	58	Ireland	115	Singapore	127
Chile	84	Israel	123	Slovenia	96
China	41	Italy	135	South Korea	90
Colombia	74	Japan	79	Spain	110
Costa Rica	33	Jordan	81	Sweden	106
Croatia	111	Kenya	31	Switzerland	108
Cuba	2	Latvia	95	Taiwan	106
Czech		Lebanon	31	Thailand	80
Republic	128	Lithuania	145	Turkey	83
Denmark	115	Luxembourg	130	Ukraine	120
Dominican	57	Malaysia	88	United Arab	173
Republic		Mexico	64	Emirates	
Ecuador	76	Morocco	64	United	118
Egypt	40	Netherlands	106	Kingdom	
Estonia	148	New Zealand	102	United States	84
Finland	115	Nigeria	27	Uruguay	90
France	90	Norway	111	Venezuela	86
Germany	118	Pakistan	48	Vietnam	27
Greece	108	Peru	55		

Source: International Telecommunication Union (ITU), "World Telecommunication Indicators Database," June 2008.

a. Penetration reflects mobile subscribers as a percentage of total population.

access the 3G network or can connect to WiFi.[43] Some analysts predict that by 2010 more than 50 percent of cellular subscribers in the United States and western Europe will access the Internet on a mobile device at least once a week. The most successful example of such phones thus far is Apple's iPhone. More than 8 million people have these handsets, with analysts conservatively predicting that, worldwide, 25 million additional units will be sold in 2009 and optimistically predicting that this number will reach 40 to 45 million.[44] The phone's popularity has attracted many imitators and has placed pressure on device manufacturers to meet newly defined consumer expectations.[45] The fact that phones will be browser based means that any payment method that works online also works on mobile phones.

—Powerful computing device. Mobile phones have become much more sophisticated computing devices over time. Around 10 percent of phones sold worldwide are so-called smart phones, with computer chips for processing, rapid-access memory, and storage. Worldwide sales of these devices are expected to maintain strong double-digit growth over the next five years. Although these phones are very powerful computers, because computing is moving to the cloud, as we discuss shortly, the client can be thin.

—Software platforms and applications. Mobile phones based on sophisticated computer hardware have operating systems that control that hardware. Most of the phones have software-platform operating systems that include both the code that runs the hardware on the phone as well as the code that provides services to applications. The competition to provide software platforms for mobile phones is extensive. The leading players at the moment by order of market share on a global basis are Symbian, Research In Motion, Windows Mobile, Mac OS X, Linux, and Palm OS. In addition, Google has recently introduced its open-source Android platform.

The primary significance of these software platforms is that they can encourage the development of the same sort of rich ecosystem of applications for mobile phones that developed for personal computers. The Apple iPhone points the way. In the two months after Apple opened its iPhone application store, more than 3,000 applications were made available there—90 percent priced at less than $10 and 600 free. Since its debut on July 11, 2008, iPhone and iPod touch users have downloaded more than 100 million applications.[46]

—Location-based technologies. An increasing number of mobile phones include GPS, which enables the network to locate the phone within a meter as long as a satellite signal can reach the phone. In 2007,

200 million mobile phones were GPS-enabled. This number is projected to reach 700 million by 2009 and 950 million by 2013.[47] There are other methods for locating the phone as well. Triangulation methods based on using several cell towers can provide a rough idea—generally within a twenty- to forty-meter range. Mobile phones also emit a unit signal that could be detected by special receivers in retail stores.

Mobile Phone Revolution in Payments

With few of these capabilities even in place, mobile phones are nonetheless substituting for plastic cards as the preferred way to make payments in several important geographic regions. Among developed countries, however, the United States is not likely to see much near-term movement in this direction. Despite the supply-side push, unresolved market constraints and consumer concerns continue to block any substantial activity.[48] Other developed countries, however, are seeing more encouraging growth. Japan and Korea lead the market, with broad contactless use now converging with mobile devices. In western Europe, efforts by companies such as Paybox in Austria and Payforit in the United Kingdom provide platforms that enable mobile payments.

In emerging countries that do not have mature payment networks, mobile payment schemes are unfolding to satisfy the needs of residents (many of whom are unbanked) rather than improving the convenience of an established process.[49] The introduction of mobile phones has revolutionized communication in many emerging economies, where landline infrastructure is often undeveloped. The mobile phone is now the key access point in many of these markets.

Safaricom's M-Pesa technology was introduced to Kenya in March 2007, for example. The service enables person-to-person money transfer and urban-to-rural remittances by Short Message Service (SMS), with currency that can be purchased at one of the many M-Pesa shops across the country. Users register for the service and, after their identity is verified, an electronic account is established that links to the customer's mobile phone number. The customer can then deposit cash with the agent that is reflected as e-money, which can then be used for trans-actions carried out over the mobile phone. Payees can then collect cash from any M-Pesa shop.[50] M-Pesa aimed to add 200,000 new customers in the first year but achieved this penetration within a month, reaching 2 million customers as of May 2008. Other schemes, such as GCASH in the Philippines and mChek in India, are providing similar services.

Another interesting development in the mobile payments arena in developing countries relates to using prepaid air minutes as a form of currency. Mobile operator Celtel in Africa reports that the transfer of air minutes by SMS is the preferred means of payment for small-scale ven-dors, amounting to its own $2 billion industry. It has become particu-larly useful in Africa, where transferring small amounts of money through banks is costly.[51]

Potential Mashups between Mobile and Payments

Much of the discussion in the payments industry has centered on using the mobile phone instead of a mag-stripe, chip-based, or contactless card. There has been great interest in whether the Japanese model points the way. This development may occur in the United States, Europe, and other parts of the world that are still card based. Mobile phones could become equipped with contactless chips, as many in Japan already are. Were such phones to become ubiquitous and people to take to the idea, it might be enough to sway merchants into investing in contactless point-of-sale terminals. It might also be that with the opportunities mobile phones provide for additional profit, some players in the ecosys-tem might subsidize contactless technology at the point of sale. It is also possible, however, that some new technology for using the mobile phone for payment will displace the contactless chip.

We believe that the current focus on the mobile phone as a form fac-tor is misplaced. It is by no means clear that it is superior to the plastic card as a payment device. People may prefer to use PIN- or signature-based cards because of security concerns. Too little thought has been given in the industry to the consumer experience at the point of sale with the mobile phone. Customers who use multiple cards will need to be able to select a card on the phone. They may find doing so both time consuming and cumbersome, depending on how the phone is designed. If they were just "smarter" than mag-stripe cards, we would not be optimistic about the widespread adoption of mobile phones for payment in countries that have an efficient card-based industry.

The mobile phone is likely to become a significant method, however, because it enables the combination of a number of transaction-related services that add value to the consumer and to the merchant. The mobile phone can easily be integrated into the consumer's shopping experience and used to locate products and services at physical stores, to compare prices, and to locate and navigate to particular stores. Consumers could also receive advertising and marketing messages related to their precise shopping experience—tailored to the store and possibly even their location within the store in real time. The phone could also store on-demand coupons. By using the location-based services on the mobile phone, it is possible to deliver coupons and advertising messages based on where the consumer is shopping at any particular moment.

Card issuers do many of these things now, but in a rudimentary way. Card issuers have loyalty programs with groups of merchants, provide rewards to consumers who shop at those merchants, and even sometimes place advertising in their monthly statements. The mobile phone would enable all these activities to be done in a more sophisticated way: to be more precisely targeted to the consumer, her shopping patterns, and current location, and to be served in real time. These mashups are facilitated by the fact that smart mobile phones have a software platform on which application programs—which embody the ultimate technology for mashups—can operate.

Cloud-Based Computing

The electronic payments industry today looks like the IT department of a conglomerate that has been kludged together from numerous mergers. The payment card system runs on two sets of rails: one for signature-based cards sponsored by the four major card networks and the other for

PIN-based cards sponsored by the PIN-debit networks. Each is based on a patchwork of systems that rely on many proprietary networks, hardware, and software platforms that have been stitched together over the years. Other parts of the electronic payments industry have their own sets of rails, including the ACH system and the electronic check-clearing system. Businesses and financial institutions must enter into point-to-point transactions for each of these payment systems using each of these rails.

With today's technology, one would design a very different system based on uniform standards and interoperable technology. As with many modern systems, much of the work would be performed in the cloud, with the Internet—subject to security issues—being used to connect the various entities that make up the electronic payments ecosystem. Participants, however, have little incentive to abandon their investments in hardware, software, and processes that work pretty well, making it more promising for entrepreneurs to improve the efficiency of the current system rather than to replace it entirely.

One can view PayPal as an early attempt to solve the problem of multiple payment rails in an online world. Buyers can plug several alternative payment methods into PayPal, including multiple signature debit and credit cards and their checking account. Sellers then can select to receive a direct ACH transfer into their accounts from PayPal. This provides a many-to-one payment method. One can think of PayPal as operating a platform for buyers, sellers, and payment method providers. PayPal is not of course neutral as to payment method providers: its business model is based on moving buyers to ACH-based transfer, which allows PayPal to avoid paying merchant fees on cards.

A much more sophisticated approach is being pursued by Denver-based IP Commerce, which has developed an operating system for the payments ecosystem that, in effect, provides a cloud-based software platform. Although they have difficult chicken and egg problems to resolve to get their platform established within the electronic payments industry, their approach is instructive because it shows how cloud-based computing could lead to a rapid increase in innovation throughout the payments industry.

The IP Commerce software platform provides for many-to-many connections. In effect, a buyer or seller who gains access to the platform's services can select among a menu of sending and receiving payment alternatives without having to install the individual connections for each one. This is similar to a PC operating system that enables the user to plug into many different peripheral devices without having to install software drivers for each one. As anyone who used personal computers twenty years ago knows, incorporating these drivers into the operating system has saved users a lot of work. Likewise, in the payments system, a standard platform for accessing multiple rails could save a great deal of time and effort. IP Commerce has been working at getting its software incorporated into the major third-party processors that handle the bulk of electronic transactions.[52]

As a software platform, IP Commerce exposes APIs, which allows developers to use IP Commerce code to provide services. PaySimple has done this. Its application enables small businesses to accept any type of electronic payments easily and cost effectively. The business can use the PaySimple software service to handle recurring bills and to generate invoices with embedded electronic payment methods. This takes only a few minutes to set up and can enable the acceptance of electronic payments online even in the absence of a merchant website. So, in this case PaySimple has developed an application (hosted in the cloud) that provides services to small business owners, relying on the IP Commerce software platform (also in the cloud) to power many of its underlying services. IP Commerce facilitates this sort of innovation by saving developers the cost and time of dealing with all of the IT complexities of the payments ecosystem. It therefore operates in much the same way as Windows. An application developer does not have to worry about dealing with a multitude of device drivers for various kinds of hardware because Windows has already done all of that work.

If this software platform, or others, became established in the electronic payments industry, it could promote a massive wave of innovation. It would become possible to develop applications that mash up various forms of payments with other technologies, including online advertising and mobile payments, without having to change much of the other parts of the payments industry.

What Mashups Mean for Consumers, Merchants, and Policymakers

Consumers constantly look for goods and services to satisfy their needs and desires at the least possible cost, even as providers of those goods and services are constantly looking for consumers to buy their wares. Value is generated when buyers and sellers find each other and engage in exchange. The buyer usually pays less than his maximum willingness to pay and therefore gets some additional benefit—what economists call consumer surplus—as a result of the transaction. The seller often gets some profit that covers not only costs but investment and risk taking as well. A diverse set of businesses and institutions in the economy facilitate the process through which buyers and sellers find and transact with each other. These include retailers, who act as intermediaries between producers and consumers, payment systems, which provide methods for paying and sometimes borrowing, and advertising and marketing, which help consumers, producers, and retailers find each other. These businesses and institutions create tremendous value by reducing frictions and transaction costs in the marketplace. It is hard to imagine a modern economy functioning at all, let alone functioning well, without well-developed distribution, payment, and information systems.

We have tried to show here that the convergence of behavioral targeting, smart mobile devices, cloud-based computing technologies, and payments could transform the shopping experience: how consumers find what they want, how producers and retailers sell consumers what they want, how the parties exchange information in this process to facilitate this matching, and how buyers pay for goods and services and sellers receive payments for those goods and services. These mashups could change the day-to-day shopping experience in profound ways. In so doing, the integration of these new technologies could create substantial value—even a fraction of the value created by modern distribution, payment, and information activities in modern economies would be a huge number.

Consumers would benefit from targeted advertising that is closely tied to what they are looking for in the physical as well as virtual worlds. Most important, consumers could benefit significantly from more useful information and more intense competition for their purchases at the point of sale. One can think of this as extending, to some degree, the easy comparison shopping available online to the physical world.

Producers of goods and services would have more efficient mechanisms for reaching consumers during their shopping excursions, targeting relevant messages to them, and assessing whether their efforts have been successful. They currently have—or, soon will have, subject to privacy concerns—these abilities in the online environment. Offline, however, the delivery of advertising is removed in time and place from the consumer's purchasing decisions, and methods for assessing how advertising messages actually influence purchasing behavior are limited.

These technologies would also enable retailers to provide a more valuable shopping environment for consumers. Indeed, some of these new technologies could deliver coupons and messages depending on where the shopper is situated within the store.

It is unclear how this convergence of technologies will occur and how it will affect the existing players in the payments ecosystem. A key consideration concerns the opportunities for consolidating the merchant and cardholder data for transactions. The banks that issue cards and handle demand deposit accounts sit on a treasure trove of data. However, those data would be far more valuable to advertisers (and to the online advertising industry) if they were pooled. That scale would increase the reach across the population and facilitate targeting of large groups of narrowly defined people.[53] Those data would be even more valuable if they could be combined with richer merchant data, which are often held by merchant processors. MasterCard and Visa could possibly facilitate combining data. But as those entities have evolved into publicly owned companies, it remains uncertain how their relationships with the banks will evolve. That uncertainty may provide opportunity for new players that do not pose competitive threats to financial institutions.

Another consideration involves the role of mobile operators. It is unclear at this point whether the mobile operators will seize some of the opportunities that are available for integrating mobile, online advertising, and payments, whether they will collaborate with other players on these technologies, or whether entrepreneurs will creatively bypass the operators whom many see as obstacles to progress. Apple is a potentially powerful player in this business because it has shifted power from the mobile operators to itself as the handset maker. Google could be important as well, although its Android software platform for mobile phones has not yet attracted a significant following. Outside the United States, mobile phone sales are often not controlled by network operators, which may facilitate the kinds of innovation we have discussed. A variety of changes in the mobile regulatory environment in the United States could encourage or discourage payments-related innovation.

Policymakers will have much to consider as this transformation of the shopping experience moves forward. Credit and debit cards have attracted an enormous amount of attention from federal and state legislators over the years. Part of this is well deserved. Some credit card lenders in this intensely competitive industry have used deceptive practices to make money. Consumers have also suffered from the theft of large quantities of data on cards stored at retailers. Meanwhile, online advertising is also attracting increased scrutiny. As noted earlier, some online advertisers have been quite aggressive in tracking consumer behavior on personal computers without the consumer's knowledge or consent.

Although policymakers should deal with these excesses, they should also recognize that the payments and online advertising industries bring tremendous value to the economy. Particularly in a period of potentially rapid and socially beneficial innovation, it is important to regulate with care, to avoid stifling that innovation—either unintentionally or to protect one or more entities threatened by it. Legitimate consumer protection concerns about deceptive lending practices, for instance, should not be used to impose unnecessary and potentially costly regulation on the performance of the payments function.

In addition, there will be legitimate concerns going forward over the use of transaction data for online advertising and over location-based methods to find out where people are. Traditional concerns over the protection of personal financial information should be carefully considered. But these need to be weighed against the value that consumers, in particular, will obtain from various new services. This is not a business versus consumer issue. To balance privacy concerns, policymakers must consider the extent to which consumer permission should be required in various settings. Should we demand that consumers specifically opt in to location-based services or to having their transaction data used for delivering advertisements and coupons to them? Or should consumers just have a clear and transparent method to opt out?[54] We believe that privacy advocates tend to overstate the risks involved with business use of consumer-specific data, but we do not deny that they raise legitimate concerns. We would only urge that policymakers recognize the potential benefits we have discussed here and proceed with care and caution to deal with the attendant privacy concerns.

One interesting feature of the current payment system environment is the variety of legal regimes governing cash, checks, cards, and other new systems of various sorts. Some have argued that the legal playing field should be leveled, or at least made somewhat less hilly, at least in part so that any new entrants would have greater certainty that they would not be disadvantaged. Although we certainly understand and appreciate the advantages of a transparent and neutral legal regime, we would once again counsel caution. The current regime, messy though it may be, has the signal merit of working well. We suggest that specific problems with the legal regime under which payment systems operate be solved only when they have been clearly identified and alternative solutions carefully explored. We are unaware of any problems and solutions that meet this standard.

Finally, we must at least touch on price regulation. Although in most areas of the U.S. economy, and of many other developed economies, price regulation is becoming a matter of only historical interest, price regulation of payment systems is emerging globally.[55] This mainly takes the form of merchant-generated pressure for reduction or elimination of the interchange fees that Visa and MasterCard have traditionally imposed on merchants and passed on to issuers. In the United States merchants have brought antitrust litigation to reduce or eliminate these fees, whereas administrative regulation of one sort or another has generally been used abroad.

With their transformation into for-profit entities, Visa and Master-Card may eliminate interchange fees at some time in the future. That is, like American Express, they can simply impose fees on merchants (or on the acquirers who deal with merchants on their behalf) and provide subsidies of various sorts to the banks that issue their cards. After all, in every successful payment system from Diners Club onward, merchants have contributed the bulk of system revenue and have been unhappy about it. The political forces that have put pressure on interchange fees will thus naturally turn to putting pressure on merchant fees directly. But if they succeed, regulation will naturally extend to merchant fees charged by all payment systems, including American Express, Discover, and any new entrants—and perhaps, to ensure that price regulation is not evaded, to other aspects of their operations.[56] If this regulation were to cascade to this extent, innovation would surely slow substantially, and the costs to consumers and businesses could be dramatic.

Notes

1. The payments industry is going through a period of creative destruction that is the result of fundamental changes in institutional arrangements, business models, and globalization over the last two years. MasterCard and Visa have transformed themselves from essentially nonprofit bank cooperatives to for-profit publicly traded firms with market values of $29.68 billion and $55.83 billion, respectively, as of September 8, 2008. A new global player has emerged with China Union Pay—a state-owned bank cooperative in China—having more than 1 billion cardholders with acceptance in twenty-seven countries and regions, rapidly expanding its footprint throughout the world. Mobile phones and related communication technologies are being used instead of traditional magnetic stripe

cards for making electronic payments in a number of countries. For more details, from the perspective of 2007, see David S. Evans, "Capitalizing on the Industry's Inflection Points," *Our Story*, pp. 45–61.

2. The term *mashup* refers to a derivative work consisting of two pieces of (generally digital) media joined together, such as a digital map overlaid with user-supplied data.

3. For further details, see Smart Card Alliance (www.smartcardalliance.org) and the NFC Forum (www.nfc-forum.org).

4. The electronic payments industry includes the credit and debit card systems, ACH-based transactions, online banking, electronic bill pay, and all other methods that provide for payment and settlement using digital money transmitted over communications networks. For much of this chapter we focus on the credit and debit card systems. Much of what we discuss, however, is relevant to the other aspects of the electronic payments industry.

5. David S. Evans and Richard Schmalensee, *Paying with Plastic*, 2nd ed. (MIT Press, 2005). For more information on payment card networks refer to Dee Hock, *One from Many* (San Francisco: Berrett-Koehler Publishers, 2005).

6. In information technology, *client* refers to a device used by an individual that can be connected to a network. A *server* is a node on a computer network that provides software and hardware services to these clients. A *thin client* is one that does not have much computing power—either processing speed, memory, or storage—often because these features are made available remotely by the server.

7. "POS Terminal Shipments Worldwide," *The Nilson Report*, no. 866 (October 2006) (www.nilsonreport.com/issues/2006/866.htm).

8. Testimony of Kim Stubna, director of Public Policy, First Data Corporation, before the House Small Business Committee, Washington, D.C.: June 2008.

9. Evans and Schmalensee, *Paying with Plastic*.

10. The survey was conducted online in August 2008 by Market Platform Dynamics. It was designed to get a general understanding of the consumer's interest in alternative form factors and transaction experiences including mobile, contactless, and various cardless solutions.

11. When asked, "When paying at the point of sale, I wish I could pay by using," 32 percent cited the mobile phone as important, 48 percent said a contactless card, and 38 percent said by not having to pull out a plastic card.

12. When asked to rank aspects of their payment experience as being important, 93 percent cited convenience, 87 percent cited a nonconfusing or easy-to-use process, and 91 percent cited a variety of payment methods.

13. This same survey asked consumers to rank their level of satisfaction with a variety of payment methods. When asked about contactless, 83 percent said that they had never tried it.

14. For a historical discussion of merchant reactions to merchant discount fees, please see Evans and Schmalensee, *Paying with Plastic*.

15. It is also anonymous, which benefits merchants and consumers for a variety of reasons, including difficulty of detection by tax authorities.

16. Market Platform Dynamics Survey of 750 small business customers in April 2008. For a complete discussion of survey results in a Market Platform Dynamics white paper, see Karen L. Webster, "The Next Payments Frontier," White Paper (Cambridge, Mass.: Market Platform Dynamics, May 2008).

17. R. Mitchell, "No Contact: Could Smart Phones Spur Contactless Payment Card Adoption?" *ComputerWorld,* June 11, 2007.

18. Federal Reserve System, "The 2007 Federal Reserve Payments Study," December 10, 2007.

19. Karen Webster, "Tap and Grow? The Case for Contactless Payments in the U.S.," PowerPoint presentation, Federal Reserve Bank of Boston, Boston, Mass., May 21, 2007.

20. For a general treatment see David S. Evans and Richard Schmalensee, *Catalyst Code* (Harvard Business School Press, 2007). For the piece that introduced the concept, see Jean-Charles Rochet and Jean Tirole, "Platform Competition in Two-Sided Markets," *Journal of the European Economic Association* 1(4)(2003): 990–1029.

21. There is considerable uncertainty over the relative costs of alternative forms of payment. See Daniel D. Garcia-Swartz, Robert W. Hahn, and Anne Layne Farrar, "The Move toward a Cashless Society: A Closer Look at Payment Instrument Economics," *Review of Network Economics* 5(2)(2006): 199–228.

22. Garcia-Swartz, Hahn, and Farrar, "The Move toward a Cashless Society."

23. See Sears Holdings Archives, www.searsarchives.com, for additional historical information.

24. Pay By Touch Press Release, "Pay By Touch Helps the World Go Walletless with Finger Scanning Payment Systems," *Business Wire,* July 22, 2005.

25. Matt Marshall, "Pay By Touch in Trouble, Founder Filing for Bankruptcy," *VentureBeat,* November 12, 2007.

26. "Octopus Cards: Statistics" (www.octopuscards.com/corporate/why/statistics/en/index.jsp).

27. "Octopus Cards: Payments" (www.octopuscards.com/corporate/application/payments/en/index.jsp#Link02).

28. Evan Ramstad, "Electronic Money Card in Hong Kong Is a Hit," *Wall Street Journal,* February 19, 2004.

29. Analyst predictions support this point. In 2004, Jupiter Research predicted that by 2006 some 151 million contactless cards would be in consumer hands and by 2009 396 million. In 2006, the firm revised these predictions, publishing 2006 penetration at 19 million and 2009 penetration at 126 million. In 2007 Packaged-Facts predicts 2009 penetration at 68 million contactless cards in consumers' hands.

30. Aite Group, "Contactless Payments and NFC in the United States: Beyond Science Fiction" (January 2008). Their reports also suggest that this number will

increase to 217,000 by 2014, representing less than 3 percent of all merchant locations.

31. According to a Jupiter Research survey of twenty-five- to thirty-four-year-old cardholders presented at CTST in Orlando, Florida, on May 14, 2008, 9.4 percent used contactless payment once a week or more.

32. Refer to the BillMeLater corporate website (www.billmelater.com).

33. Tempo, however, has moved to providing a platform for decoupled debit cards—cards various parties can issue that tap into the consumer's checking account via ACH—and Revolution Money has started a P2P payment service online.

34. *SKU* is a unique numeric identifier assigned to a product and used to track inventory.

35. David S. Evans, "The Economics of the Online Advertising Industry," *Review of Network Economics* 7(3)(2008): 359–91.

36. Strategy Analytics reports that worldwide mobile ad spending will increase from $1 billion in 2008 to $2.4 billion in 2009. Other analysts are as bullish, citing the number of people worldwide with mobile phones, especially those in emerging countries, where the mobile phone is a proxy for a PC.

37. That involves looking at search histories, web visits, web e-mail, and possibly correlating those data with other sources of data.

38. The Senate Commerce Committee held hearings in Washington, D.C., on online advertising and privacy (for a summary of that testimony, see www.searchengineland.com/080710-090207.php). The European Parliament held similar hearings in January 2008.

39. After a lot of public controversy and a campaign on Facebook mounted by Moveon.org, Facebook has since changed this system to be a strictly opt-in.

40. See Cellfire's website (www.cellfire.com).

41. See Tom Eisenmann, "Inside the Google Money Machine," *Harvard Business School*, February 1, 2008.

42. Nick Jones, "Important Mobile and Wireless Market Directions 2008 to 2012," *Gartner, Inc.* (2008).

43. Ibid.

44. Piper Jaffray Companies prediction.

45. Jason Chapman, Carolina Milanesi, and David A. Willis, "Key Trends in Mobile Devices, 2008–2009," *Gartner, Inc.* (2008).

46. Jason Ankeny, "iPhone App Store Tops 100 Million Downloads," *FierceMobileContent*, September 10, 2008.

47. George Perros, "GPS-Enabled Mobile Devices," *ABI Research* (2008).

48. On September 25, 2008, Visa introduced mobile payment services via Google's Android platform and Nokia by yearend 2008. Visa has publicized that the service will include initiatives such as mobile applications for Android that will allow Chase Visa cardholders to receive mobile notifications following making a

transaction, receive offers from merchants using Android's LBS technology, as well as make contactless payments, remote payments, and money transfer. Jason Ankeny, "Visa Expands M-Payment Service via Android, Nokia," *FierceMobile-Content*, September 25, 2008.

49. Frost & Sullivan, "Social Impact of Mobile Telephony in Latin America" (GSM Association, 2006) (www.gsmlaa.org/files/content/0/94/Social%20Impact%20of%20Mobile%20Telephony%20in%20Latin%20America.pdf).

50. Olga Morawczynski, "Surviving in the 'Dual System': How M-PESA is Fostering Urban-to-Rural Remittances in a Kenyan Slum," University of Edinburgh, 2008.

51. Associated Press, "Cell Phones Reshaping Africa," CNN.com, October 17, 2005.

52. The IP Commerce software is also included in Microsoft Office, so that small businesses that use Office for invoicing can incorporate payment functionality—such as sending or receiving money electronically—into their invoices.

53. Because only a small fraction of consumers click on ads, advertisers require large numbers of viewers to warrant the cost of launching an advertising campaign.

54. Richard Thaler and Cass Sunstein, *Nudge* (Yale University Press, 2008).

55. Courts or competition authorities have determined that interchange fees as set by card schemes are unlawful in the European Community, Australia, Spain, and Poland. Investigations and lawsuits are proceeding in many other jurisdictions. The U.S. Congress is considering legislation to regulate interchange fees. U.S. merchants have filed a private antitrust lawsuit against MasterCard and Visa that seeks to eliminate the interchange fee.

56. The late James W. McKie, professor emeritus of economics at the University of Texas–Austin, introduced the term *tar baby effect* to regulation to explain what happens when an agency applies a regulation, perhaps a defensible one, to one aspect of business, only to have the result not be what it had hoped, and then seeks to implement additional regulation to correct what did not occur with the initial regulation.

DRAZEN PRELEC

4

Consumer Behavior and the
Future of Consumer Payments

A billboard ad for a prepaid long-distance telephone card once ran the slogan "Now you can call your loved ones and not think about how much it costs." The ad points to a basic dilemma in consumer attitudes to payment. From a pleasure standpoint, one would like to minimize thought of payment. From a decision standpoint, however, one definitely needs to know how much something costs. The dilemma may be expressed by saying that the consumer wants to know the cost of consumption, but does not want to think unduly about it.

In this chapter I take up the question of what consumers might ideally want from payment arrangements. Granted, to speak of payments as providing any positive benefits at all may seem unusual. It is more natural to think of payments as a necessary evil that financial and technological innovations can perhaps mitigate. On the financial side, these innovations can give consumers more flexibility about how they will pay, thus more control over time and risk. Technology, in turn, can make individual transactions more convenient, fast, and secure.

These are not insignificant objectives. They are largely concerned, though, with removing the imperfections of traditional modes of payment. If there is a utopian vision here, it is an essentially negative one, of total financial liquidity and effortless, instant transactions. The implicit model of consumer preference is elementary in the extreme, emphasizing obvious dimensions such as cost, risk, security, privacy, and speed.

A glance at key trends in the use of different payment instruments should cast doubt on the adequacy of this circumscribed conception of consumer needs. Among the major categories, debit cards have been the fastest growing segment, and as of 2006 have displaced credit cards as the top payment method by total number of transactions. Credit cards, however, have multiple advantages and no countervailing disadvantages relative to debit cards: they provide a short-term interest-free loan, they increase liquidity, giving the option of costless conversion of the balance into uncollateralized debt, and they are much more likely to be bundled with attractive reward programs.[1] Therefore, on financial grounds, it is hard to understand the appeal of the debit card.[2]

Similar considerations apply to prepaid cards, which function like a debit card except that the funds are not linked to a bank account. Instead, the consumer preloads a certain amount on the card at activation time, and the purchases are then deducted from the balance until no funds remain (most, but not all, cards can be reloaded). These cards, which are often marketed as a "bank account in your wallet," provide even less liquidity than debit cards, yet are projected to be the fastest growing segment over the next five years.

It is hard to ascribe the success of either method, debit or prepaid, to dramatic financial or technological innovations. Rather, experimentation with different payment methods eventually generated products tapping into overlooked but evidently important consumer needs.[3] In the remainder of this chapter, I speculate on what these needs might be. These speculations are inspired by recent experimental findings in behavioral economics and by inferences from marketplace phenomena. I do not discuss technological developments per se; instead, my goal is to outline broad psychological goals that are important when ideas for new technologies and mechanisms are considered.

By payment arrangements I refer to the full set of financial obligations incurred with a purchase, not just to the properties of individual transactions. One can, after all, pay for goods and services many ways.

In a retail setting one has the choice between paying in cash or using a card. Among cards, there are again many possibilities—credit cards, debit cards, charge cards, stored value cards, prepaid cards, and others. Online purchases also present payment options, for example, between card charges, electronic currencies, and the old-fashioned paper bill (BillMeLater). In many product categories choices are offered between flat and variable rates, between prix fixe and à la carte offerings, and between owning and renting. A producer can charge separately for the hardware and the software, for the basic model and for any options, for the initial version and for upgrades, not to speak of discounts, surcharges, frequent-flyer miles, and such. From the perspective of the producer, the selection of a pricing arrangement presents such opportunities for invention and creative refinement as to make the task more an integral part of product design than a textbook pricing exercise.

A theory of design is a formulation of general principles rather than a set of quantitative rules. Such principles should address the question of what consumers want from payment arrangements beyond the obvious financial and transactional benefits. I venture here a preliminary assessment, namely, that they want

—to enjoy goods and services as if they were free,

—to be able to justify any payments with specific and salient benefits, and

—to preserve financial responsibility and self-control.

This is a provisional definition of the core benefits of payment arrangements. These benefits are not naturally aligned, and arrangements that cater to one often do so at the expense of another. The challenging design objective is to reconcile them. This is where technology might help.

Removing the Moral Tax on Consumption

The observation that payments take some of the glow off consumption is a commonplace. To refresh our intuitions let us perform a simple thought experiment: imagine a lavish dinner, with the best possible food, wonderful service, and in the company of a few favorite friends.

However, you are personally responsible for the full cost of the dinner—perhaps beforehand the group drew straws to determine who would pay, and you got the short one. The total price is expected to be greater than any single dinner bill you have ever absorbed (take whatever figure comes to mind and then double it). Let us call this Scenario A.

Now, imagine that a few days before the planned dinner, the restaurant called to inform you that—as part of a special promotion celebrating its recently acquired third Michelin star—the establishment will pick up the full bill. The dinner is complimentary. Let us call this Scenario B.

The critical question is whether there is any reason to expect a difference between how the dinner experience will feel under the two scenarios. If your intuition is that it will feel exactly the same—because the consumption components are identical, the same food and the same company, after all—then you qualify as a rational consumer. In my experience, posing this question informally, it is extremely rare to encounter a rational consumer of this description. There is instead a robust majority opinion that the free scenario will allow for greater satisfaction, especially as one moves from dessert to coffee and the mint tray arrives without the customary check. The minor financial windfall created by the phone call bleeds over into the dinner experience (to be fair, there is also a minority opinion that the dinner will actually feel better in the first scenario because the high cost will "concentrate the mind").

Analyzing this from a utilitarian perspective, one could conclude that if the complimentary dinner experience measures up to u utils, then full payment experience is diminished, say, by $-\Delta u$. This may be obvious but, from a rational perspective, is quite odd. When a person pays for the dinner, the price represents an opportunity cost—perhaps it means no new sport coat this season. But this does not explain why the forgone sport coat should hover in the background and spoil the dinner experience. The consumer seems to pay twice, first with the necessary opportunity cost (no coat) and then with an entirely unnecessary *moral tax* on consumption, to the tune of Δu.[4]

The moral tax represents the psychological intrusion of payments into consumption, robbing the consumer of some portion of rightful enjoyment. The rational consumer, in contrast, should enjoy all goods and services as if they were free.[5] To him prices are simply a counter, with no hedonic consequences.

The presence of the moral tax creates a new motive, which is to structure payments in such a way as to minimize the hedonic loss. Here are some strategies that work.[6]

Prepayment

A simple yet effective device for reducing the moral tax is to prepay for things. Consumers will readily reveal such a preference in questionnaires.[7]

> Imagine that you are planning a one-week vacation to the Caribbean, six months from now. The vacation will cost $1,200. You have two options for financing the vacation: six monthly payments of $200 each during the six months either before the vacation (A) or after you return (B).

Most consumers (63 percent) prefer option A, in spite of the significant penalty in forgone interest. However, the preference for prepayment is not always present, as shown by the next example.

> Imagine that, six months from now, you are planning to purchase a clothes washer and dryer for your new residence. The two machines together will cost $1,200. You have two options for financing: six monthly payments of $200 each during the six months either before (A) or after (B) the washer-dryer arrives.

Here, most consumers (76 percent) prefer option B. In general, with consumer durables people prefer to buy on an installment plan, with payments starting when the durable is delivered.

The financial decision is identical in both examples. What then accounts for the shift in preference? When probed further, consumers say that the reason for prepayment in the vacation question is to protect the vacation experience from thoughts of cost. A second reason is that the payments themselves feel better if they are made in advance of the vacation. In other words, they are an investment toward the vacation. By contrast, payments made after the vacation feel naked—not covered by any future benefits.

The situation with the washer-dryer is different. It is a utilitarian product that provides little experiential satisfaction; the amount of pleasure exposed to the moral tax is low. The washer-dryer is also a durable, so the payments can be seen as a contribution to an ongoing series of benefits, rather than as a charge for past consumption.

Feelings about consumption and payments reflect a double-entry mental (psychological) accounting system, in which feelings about payments are influenced by what these payments are for, and feelings about consumption are influenced by associated payments.[8] There is cross talk between consumption and payments; they cannot be analyzed independently. Moreover, the mental accounting system is *prospective*, emphasizing future events and largely ignoring past ones. Prospective accounting creates two distinct reasons to prepay: payments feel like an investment and consumption feels free.[9]

The desire for prepayment is a robust but still too little appreciated and understood phenomenon. It has gone unrecognized partly because of a long-standing view of consumers as myopic, self-indulgent creatures, and partly because the decision to prepay for consumption is often made indirectly—for instance, by choosing to own rather than rent a product.[10] Imagine, for example, that you are thinking about purchasing a tuxedo, on the assumption that your social activities require black tie dress about once every few years or so. Setting aside the purely financial considerations, might you not say to yourself, "Let me make this one-time investment and never again have to think about the cost of dressing up for these parties." Even in the absence of an actual prepayment mechanism, consumers can capture some of the same hedonic benefits by mentally setting aside or budgeting a requisite amount; many existing payment practices can be understood precisely as facilitators of such a mental prepayment. With a prix fixe menu, for instance, one can psychologically absorb the costs before the food arrives at the table and enjoy the dinner as if it were prepaid.

Buffer Currencies

Prepayment carries several obvious disadvantages. One is opportunity cost in forgone interest. Another is that prepayment is typically irreversible, committing the consumer to items or activities that may later prove undesirable. Are there payment methods that provide the psychological benefits of prepayment but preserve flexibility in making decisions?

Token currencies, such as casino chips or the beads used to pay for drinks at Club Med vacation resorts, let the consumer purchase in advance without requiring him or her to specify the basket of goods for which the tokens will be exchanged. Purchase decisions can still be made on the fly but consumption feels relatively free because the currency itself has been prepaid. I refer to these currencies as *hedonic buffers* because by interposing themselves between real money and consumption, they protect consumption from the moral tax. Moreover, the acquisition of the buffer currency has aspects of an investment.

Prepaid cards are relatively new and a promising mechanism for creating any number of buffer currencies. The balance on a prepaid card is in principle completely fungible. Yet the cards provide a soft constraint in that the funds are earmarked for a particular category of expenses. The earmarking contributes to the feeling that subsequent consumption is prepaid. For example, travel cards provide the psychological benefits of a fully prepaid vacation package without locking in any of the details. Gift cards and employee incentive (reward) cards have the same characteristics. They preserve the moral-tax advantage of a gift (guilt-free enjoyment), but give the recipient flexibility about how to spend the money.[11]

Frequency Programs

Frequency programs such as frequent flyer miles are another form of buffering currency. Products acquired with the currency are often perceived—and indeed officially designated—as free, such as a free ticket or a free upgrade obtained with miles. In reality, they are only prepaid, not free.

The perception that a business-class or first-class upgrade is free removes the moral tax from what otherwise is likely to feel like a complete extravagance. The passenger who has paid for the upgrade out of his or her pocket will be tempted to scrutinize the experience to see whether it indeed justifies the price. Such scrutiny highlights the moral tax, leading to even lower satisfaction. In contrast, the free upgrade passenger can savor the flight luxuries without giving thought to their cost.

A distinctive feature of the reward program currency is that it must be earned over time. From the moral tax perspective, this creates a double benefit. First, the original purchases acquire the secondary characteristics of a savings plan. At the moment of purchase, consumers can choose to concentrate on the increments to the buffer currency balance and ignore the reductions in their real currency account. Because it is difficult if not impossible to convert dollars into the buffer currency directly, purchase transactions become the only available method for building up a buffer balance. Second, consumers who might otherwise feel guilty about purchasing a luxury item will feel less guilt if the item was in effect earned through a patient accumulation of previous purchases. The guilt-reducing aspect of frequency programs has been nicely shown in recent studies. Ran Kivetz and Itamar Simonson, for example, found that as the effort requirement in the program increases, consumer preferences about how to cash in on the reward points shift toward luxuries.[12] In effect, the consumer is gradually building up a license to indulge, and the size of the license is proportional to the invested effort.

Bundling

Payment arrangements vary in how tightly they link costs and consumption. We refer to this as the level of *financial coupling* of purchases and payments.[13] Coupling is a generalization of time discounting, and takes into account not only the time interval between two events but also the strength and clarity of the causal links between them. Like time discounting, a lower level of coupling will also reduce the moral tax. Several factors affect coupling.

Returning to the lavish dinner example, let us vary the scenario one more time, and imagine that the dinner is included as part of a weekend getaway package for you and your friends. The total cost, for which you again are unfortunately responsible, would in this case be even larger and include hotel and other expenses. The contribution of the dinner to this total cost is not known, however. We can say that when the check arrives it requires only an endorsing signature but does not present a specific dollar figure. How would this affect the enjoyment of the dinner?

Faced with this situation, most people feel that the dinner experience would fall somewhere between the previous two cases—not as good as the free dinner but definitely better than the dinner with known cost. It is as if the ambiguity in the imputation of cost to the dinner is resolved in the direction of a lower figure and lower moral tax. A priori, one might think that risk aversion would create greater sensitivity to ambiguous costs, but that does not seem to be the case as long as the total cost of the package is known. Moral taxes need not add up. This argues for all-inclusive over à la carte pricing, where the cost of individual components and options is indicated separately.

Fixed Payment Plans and Subscriptions

The same principle applies to decisions between fixed versus variable payment plans for services. This can be seen in responses to a question about health clubs.

> Mr. A and Mr. B both joined health clubs. Mr. A's club charged a fixed fee for each month of usage. Mr. B's charged an hourly fee. By chance, both men used the health club about the same amount, and both ended up getting a bill for the same amount at the end of the month. Who enjoyed himself more while using the club?

From an economic standpoint, the correct inference from the facts as stated is that Mr. B should enjoy the club more. In deciding whether to visit the club on any given day, both individuals should balance the pleasure of exercise against the total opportunity costs, which include time, travel, and fees. Because only Mr. B has to pay the hourly fee, his opportunity cost is higher, implying that the utility he derives from an hour at the club is higher than that Mr. A derives. Yet, in our survey most people (by a 3:1 margin) judged that Mr. A would enjoy the club more.[14]

A scrupulous accountant in the role of Mr. A might amortize the fixed fee over the total number of monthly visits to the health club, and arrive (in this case) at the same per visit cost as Mr. B, and suffer the same moral tax. But how many consumers will go through this mental amortization process? Of course, if the number of visits is low, one might reach the conclusion that the club is not worth the expense. But the individual visits would still be protected from the moral tax.

The moral tax involves only costs that are direct causal consequences of a consumption decision, not those that set up the consumption opportunity. The tax targets the final element in the causal chain and largely ignores the preceding ones. Therefore, payment arrangements that create zero marginal costs will support a feeling that consumption is free, and sustain higher satisfaction levels.

Accounting for Costs, and Minimizing Pain of Payment

We now turn to the other half of the consumer's double-entry mental accounting system, which deals with feelings generated by the payment transaction.

Eliminating Uncovered Payments

The success of the Netflix subscription plan for DVD rentals is a textbook example of the importance of both sides of the system. Currently, the most popular Netflix plan charges a monthly fee and allows a subscriber to rent up to three DVDs at a time, with unlimited exchanges. This minimizes the moral tax on consumption, because the DVD is mentally prepaid and the marginal cost of watching an extra movie is zero.

However, the plan also provides a benefit on the payment side, at least relative to standard rental arrangements. On the Netflix plan, subscribers hang on to the DVDs for as long as they like and no late fees apply. With standard rental arrangements, when consumers return DVDs late and incur the fee, it may be due to simple neglect (*bounded rationality*) rather than to a deliberate purchase of an extra night of viewing. For the forgetful consumer on the standard plan, the late fee is an *uncovered payment*, that is, a payment for which the consumer cannot identify any salient benefit (one could associate an option-value benefit with the late fee, but it is not likely most consumers would do so). By eliminating these annoying payments, Netflix increases average satisfaction.

The Netflix plan illustrates a more general lesson, namely, that it may be better to solve the bounded rationality problem than to try to exploit it. Consumers are typically better at deciding about which of several items to consume than at deciding whether it is worth consuming an item of a certain type at a given price. Netflix allows consumers to concentrate on picking the right film and thus eliminates the second decision—whether watching any movie on a given night is worth the marginal cost. Moreover, consumers tend to be absent-minded and often forget to return items when due. Although one could craft a strategy around maximizing rental volume and unintended late fees, the superior approach, in this case at least, is to forfeit these traditional sources of revenue and cultivate long-run happiness with the service.

Overaccounting

As mentioned earlier, mental accounting terms do not need to add up, which opens the door to counting benefits multiple times. Pennies-a-day payment plans probably exploit mental double-counting. Because the product is typically indivisible, nothing mentally corresponds to the product fragment being purchased with a single payment. The consumer can thus easily exaggerate the contribution of each payment to the final price.

Transaction Coupling

An important psychological difference among payment instruments is how tightly they couple consumption and payment. The causal link is most direct with a cash or debit card purchase—the money disappears when the purchase is made. Payment by check imposes a delay, but the causal link is otherwise equally straightforward. With a charge card, there is a single bill at the end of the month; payment for a given purchase is both delayed and combined with payments for other items. Hence the level of coupling is somewhat weaker because no single item is responsible for the total.

For a credit card, the connection becomes even more blurred, especially if a balance is maintained on the card from month to month. In principle, one could take each payment and decide how to apply it to the items previously charged on the card. This exercise would allow a person to cross items off the list as they are paid off. It is more realistic to assume that a consumer who maintains a balance is not aware which items are responsible for the total or which items should be considered paid for.

Weak coupling may explain consumers' striking ambivalence toward credit card usage. At the moment of purchase, the moral tax is small because the payments can be delayed, indefinitely if need be. Moreover, because payments will be combined with those for other goods, no single transaction or set of transactions necessarily constitutes payment for that particular item. In this sense, the item may seem free.

At the same time, when the consumer writes a check clearing some part of the credit card bill, the expense cannot be traced to any individual purchases. This makes credit card payments exceptionally distasteful—it is not obvious what is being received in exchange for the payment except the ability to continue using the card. Indeed, a survey of attitudes to payment found that a credit card bill (of $300) is ranked as most painful of many different categories of bills, even topping parking tickets or dental bills (all for the same amount of $300).[15] It may also explain why credit cards are paradoxically judged to be a costly method of payment, more costly than debit.[16]

Preserving Self-Control

We now turn to the third proposed benefit of pricing arrangements, namely, the desire to preserve accountability and self-control. Here, credit cards are often raised as a problematic payment method. The liberating effect of credit cards on purchase behavior is consistent with cross-sectional evidence,[17] and has been documented in at least two controlled experiments.[18] In one, MBA students had the opportunity to bid for basketball tickets to a sold-out Celtics game—the final game of the regular season, with playoff home-court advantage hinging on the outcome.[19] The auction used the incentive compatible second-price sealed-bid format. Half the participants received a bidding sheet that requested payment in cash within a twenty-four-hour grace period, and the other half received a sheet requesting payment by major credit card. Subjects were not aware of the existence of the different sets of instructions.

Bids in the credit card condition were on average twice as high as those in the cash condition ($61 versus $20, with median values of $41 and $25, respectively). The difference cannot be explained by liquidity constraints in the cash condition. On that hypothesis, cash condition subjects should have been willing to use their credit card to purchase cash from the experimenter at a 100 percent markup. This is simply not credible. It is interesting also that the result failed to be replicated with a more fungible prize of stated value (a $175 gift certificate to a local restaurant), suggesting that the credit card willingness-to-pay premium is not constant across types of goods.[20]

Tickets to a sold-out game are a relative indulgence with an ambiguous market value. The usual norms on what is reasonable to pay may not apply, leaving the subject a great deal of freedom to come up with a reasonable figure. In these situations, where market prices are not known, consumer valuations of products are easily influenced by irrelevant variables, such as hypothetical anchoring questions.[21] Indeed, consumer valuation for a product is better conceptualized as an interval instead of a point value. If the price falls outside of that interval, the decision becomes cognitive and relatively easy, that is, reachable without an introspective balancing of pleasures and pains. When the price is within the interval, the consumer falls back on an intrinsically unstable hedonic calculus. That payment is by credit card may assuage some of the sting of payment, pushing the valuation upward.

From the bidding data in the basketball ticket experiment, one cannot conclude that the individuals in the credit card condition are bidding too high; it is just as possible that the cash bids are too low relative to the utility that the game would provide. There could be an irrational pain associated with physically handing over cash. Notably, although the credit card bids went as high as $325, no cash bid exceeded $100. Regardless of which group is in error, it is clear that individuals do not fully appreciate the extent to which their valuation can be influenced by payment method. Again, we take it as self-evident that one could not sell cash for credit card charges at a 100 percent premium, at least not to MBA students.

If the payment method works its magic under the radar, there are two important implications. First is that consumers who accumulate excessive card balances may not initially appreciate that anything has changed in their spending patterns. They may think that they are maintaining the same criteria for purchases, yet see the balances inexplicably increase. For such consumers, a useful experiment would be to switch to cash transactions for a trial period without adopting any other self-control measure, and see if this produces any change in expenditure patterns. Second, unaware of the credit card effect, consumers may not reveal the need for an alternative payment method in interviews. This may explain why very few mention self-control to explain their use of debit cards.[22]

Addictive Consumption

Can credit card use become an addiction? To qualify as such it would have to meet two conditions. First, it would have to be a compulsion, that is, a behavior a person indulges in knowing that it is harmful. Second, it would have to tap a brain mechanism common to substance addictions. Judging from the availability of self-help programs, credit cards are indeed a compulsion for at least some of the population. There is little hard evidence bearing on the second condition, however. In a provocative early study, which was unfortunately never followed up, subjects were asked to indicate how much they were hypothetically willing to pay for various products, which were presented on a computer screen.[23] Brochures showing credit card logos lay on a table within view of a control group, but were unrelated to the products being evaluated. Subjects who inquired about them were told that they were left over from a previous experiment. The presence of the brochures led to higher product valuations (by a factor of two), and faster response times, both effects indicating a greater motivation to purchase.

A psychologist would see here the fingerprints of a classical (Pavlovian) conditioning process. The credit card shopper has experienced many occasions on which the physical stimuli associated with the card (look, feel) anticipated the purchases. If the act of purchase produces a pleasant "rush," then, by the conditioning process, the anticipatory stimuli will eventually trigger an opposite and unpleasant physiological response, which we experience as a craving. The only way to suppress the craving is to complete the purchase.[24]

Neuroscience of Shopping

We are only beginning to understand the neuroscience of consumer decisionmaking, and this is not the place for a review of neuroeconomics.[25] However, one recent brain imaging study of shopping bears mentioning.[26] In the study, subjects faced a series of purchase decisions while their brain activity was imaged with the fMRI scanner. Each purchase decision began with a computer display of an actual product, followed a few seconds later by the price. The subjects then indicated, by button press, whether they would choose to purchase the product at that price. The time between the product and the price presentations allowed separate measurement of brain activity, responding to the product and to the price. The profile of activity triggered by product presentation roughly mimicked the patterns observed earlier with presentations of rewarding stimuli (activation in the brain dopaminergic networks, encompassing the striatum and the medial prefrontal cortex).

Of more interest is the profile of activation in response to price. Presentation of high prices generated activity in the insular cortex, which has been otherwise implicated in processing of pain, aversion, and disgust. The magnitude of the insular response in the shopping task was proportional to the difference between the posted price and the value of the product (as assessed separately, outside the fMRI scanner). In other words, prices in excess of what the consumer was willing to pay elicited an aversive response that could be measured by the brain scan, which is consistent with the pain-of-paying hypothesis.

A Functional Explanation

Why are consumers exposed to the pain of paying? The most likely explanation is that the pain is there to shore up self-control mechanisms. Self-control is of course a hallmark virtue of human character and is defined as the ability to avoid temptations and to make choices that promote more distant goals. Willingness of the tired body to exercise and of the tired mind to undertake another hour of work are two examples of positive self-control—the tolerance of short-term pain in return for a larger but more remote and uncertain gain. Turning down a chocolate dessert or an attractive purchase opportunity are examples of negative self-control—avoiding immediate and certain satisfaction to preserve broader financial objectives or self-esteem.[27] Both modes are central to normal adult functioning, and several categories of psychological disturbance—impulsivity, addiction, and psychopathy—appear to be intimately associated with chronic lack of self-control.[28]

Although the mechanisms that support self-control are not completely understood, what is evident—and highly relevant to the design of payment arrangements—is that successful exercise of self-control can exact a steep price. Self-control requires energy, drawing on the same bodily resources as tasks requiring physical effort. Self-control is more likely to break down when these resources are depleted through fatigue. Conversely, exercising self-control (for example, by resisting tasty food) actually makes people physically weaker, as measured by how hard they can squeeze a handgrip.[29] Many of the strategies people use to exercise self-control have a dark side. Excessive control of appetite or sexual feelings can produce a permanent loss of the capacity for pleasure (anorexia or frigidity, for example). Strict personal rules raise the stakes on minor actions, leading to behavioral rigidity and compulsion.[30]

Consumer finance is one of the major arenas in which the individual's self-control is put to the test.[31] The benefits of the purchase decision are typically more immediate than the costs and are also more salient—the costs are only an opportunity cost, and people rarely know exactly how they would use the money saved by declining the purchase. In fact, merely reminding people that refraining from buying a product for $x will essentially give them $x to spend for other purchases reduces purchase rates in an experimental setting.[32]

Pain of paying and the moral tax can be seen as mechanisms for redressing the imbalance in the decisional balance sheet, which would otherwise be chronically tilted in favor of the decision to purchase. Like most taxes, it provides a second-best solution, placing a deadweight burden on the consumer.[33] Indeed, a recent large survey of consumer attitudes to spending found that more consumers confess to being too tight (in the sense of not spending on "things they should spend it on") rather than too loose (in the sense of spending "when they would do better not to spend").[34] The miser who is unable to enjoy even the smallest luxuries is of course a stock figure; what is surprising, in light of the current press attention to consumer overspending, is that there are so many closet misers in the general population.

Hedonic or Economic Efficiency: The Big Trade-Off

In designing new payment methods, it is natural to focus on the transaction. Usually the method involves some innovation in the transaction process, for example, integrating transactional capabilities with other electronic media and devices. This feature captures the imagination and forms the foundation for an advertising campaign. Moreover, from the corporate point of view, transactions drive revenue, making transaction volume the first and most obvious metric to watch.

For these reasons, it is easy to overlook the fact that for the consumer, the transaction is only a means, not the end; it is the cutlery, not the meal. The quality of the transaction is entangled with the quality of the decisions the transaction implements. There is evidence, both from the field and from the lab, that a payment method is not just an instrument for carrying out a purchase decision reached on some independent grounds, but actually a causal ingredient in the decision. If a payment mechanism chronically encourages poor decisions, consumer enthusiasm for the method will wane. At the same time, consumers may not be fully aware of or able to explain why their transaction preferences are changing.

In upholding decision quality as a criterion, it may seem that we are broadening the canvas too much. How is one to define decision quality without imposing paternalistic preferences? This is obviously a thorny issue, and any proposal is bound to be speculative. I suggested earlier that the ideal payment method would provide the consumer with three key benefits: first, reduce or eliminate the moral tax, allowing the consumer to enjoy goods and services as if they were free; second, provide an accounting function, letting the consumer justify any payment with specific benefits; and, third, encourage an appropriate level of spending, that is, it should preserve financial responsibility and bolster self-control.

There are two tensions in play here. One is that arrangements that reduce the moral tax tend also to make it more difficult to track expenses, reducing financial accountability. The second is that if the moral tax is essential for self-control, successfully eliminating the tax will automatically encourage overspending.

Many of the payment arrangements considered in this chapter may be construed as ad hoc attempts to solve the moral tax problem. All such attempts run up against an underlying trade-off between economic efficiency—understood as more liquidity, more options, lower costs—and hedonic efficiency, understood as the satisfaction or utility extracted

Table 4-1. *The Fundamental Trade-off in Pricing Arrangements*

Promoting hedonic efficiency	Promoting economic efficiency
Owning	Renting or leasing
Prepayment, investing	Postpayment, borrowing
Gift rewards, earmarking	Cash rewards, liquidity
Multiple currencies and accounts	Single currency, one comprehensive account
Flat rate plans, subscriptions	Fee-per-use plans
Prix fixe, bundled options	À la carte, unbundled options
Hidden taxes and fees, public goods	Explicit taxes and fees, market goods

from a given product or experience. Simply put, economic efficiency is about selecting the best option, and hedonic efficiency is about getting the most out of whatever option you do select, or whatever option is selected on your behalf.

Table 4-1 presents contrasting pairs of arrangements, so that one element in the pair (the left column) enhances hedonic efficiency, and the other (the right column) economic.[35] The table glosses over who is responsible for choosing the arrangement; in some cases it is the consumer (owning versus renting), in some cases the producer (frequency reward plans), and in some government policy (the scope of free public amenities).

At the top of the list is the choice of whether to purchase an item or simply rent or lease. Economic efficiency argues for renting if the rental market offers similar terms. Ownership has many economic disadvantages, starting with its relative irreversibility. One's future tastes are hard to forecast and circumstances change. It is costly to dispose of or sell an object that no longer serves your needs. However, possessions are not subject to the same moral tax as rentals. If you take your own car for an afternoon drive in the country, time and gas are the only costs that might come to mind. If you rent, the rental bill will surely be factored into the equation.

The common characteristics of the economic arrangements (column 2) are that they simultaneously expand options, and by making marginal costs explicit and easy to track, encourage more rational choice among these options. In contrast, the arrangements in column 1 introduce constraints and complications that restrict options and, by eliminating marginal costs, give rise to inefficient consumer decisions. What the hedonic arrangements accomplish in return is to provide relief from the moral tax. Their proliferation and popularity in spite of their economic drawbacks testify to the reality of the moral tax. The desire to avoid the tax finds a comprehensive expression in the socialist utopia in which all goods are dispensed freely.[36]

Framed this way, the dilemma appears difficult to resolve. The illiquidity of frequent flyer miles is precisely the feature that sustains the illusion that a flight obtained with those miles is free. If miles could be bought and sold without restriction, then the distinction between the two currencies would collapse, as would the notion of a free upgrade. The blocked exchange seems essential to the hedonic benefit.

Yet this general conclusion may be too pessimistic. One can imagine ways of removing, or at least displacing outward, the trade-off between our two opposed efficiency criteria. A useful analogy can be made with the strategies and arguments developed by the soft paternalism movement, which has gained a great deal of attention in public policy discussions recently.[37] Soft paternalism, also known as libertarian or asymmetric paternalism, replaces prohibitions and mandates with the judicious construction of a choice architecture that biases decisions in a desired direction without abridging ultimate freedom of choice. The canonical design challenge is the formulation of the default option, which passive or confused individuals tend to adopt. When this formulation is handled well, the change in behavior can be dramatic.[38]

In the context of payment arrangements, the analogous goal would be to translate the hard constraints embodied in hedonic arrangements into discretionary soft constraints, which the consumer could cancel if needed. The distinction between renting and owning could be finessed by hybrid arrangements, such as time sharing and renting to own, and by the increasing availability of electronic secondhand markets. Payment mechanisms should facilitate the selection of entire consumption policies, such as subscriptions and flat rate plans, allowing quick adjustment to more optimal policies in response to changes in consumption rates. Prepayment should be made easy and reversible, with compensation provided for lost interest. Whenever possible, transactions should sustain the experience of investment toward future consumption.

The ultimate paternalistic goal here is easy to state but not easy to achieve. It is to promote decisions that the consumer would, on reflection, recognize as correct, that is, in his or her best interests. We discussed the three core benefits of payment arrangements as if they are logically separate. Psychologically, however, it likely that the third one—the desire for self-control and the desire to escape the anxieties associated with lack of self-control—provides the motivational fuel for the first two. A person who makes consumption decisions in perfect confidence that these decisions are right is probably also exempt from moral tax, and from the pain of paying.[39] Whether new technologies in payment mechanisms will be able to secure this goal remains to be seen.

Notes

1. Marc A. Fusaro, "Debit vs. Credit: A Model of Self-Control with Evidence from Checking Accounts," Working Paper (Greenville, N.C.: East Carolina University, 2008).

2. There is evidence that consumers who maintain a credit card balance ("revolvers") are more likely to use a debit card, even if they are not close to the limit on their credit card balances. The debit card preference among revolvers is taken as evidence of rational price sensitivity, because such consumers face unavoidable interest on any new credit card charges. Jonathan Zinman, "Debit or Credit?" Working Paper (Hanover, N.H.: Dartmouth College, 2006). But, if the consumer has enough funds to cover the debit card payment, why does he or she not apply those funds to reduce the credit card balance?

3. The headline text for the prepaid card section on the consumer advisory website Creditcards.com reads as follows: "Prepaid debit cards and prepaid credit cards can help you control your spending. A reloadable debit card allows you to only spend up to the amount you have pre-deposited into the account. If you tend to overspend or would like to control your spending then a pre-paid debit card or prepaid credit card could be a good card for you" (www.creditcards.com/prepaid.php).

4. The moral tax is a symptom of a more general psychological tendency to experience opportunity costs as real pain. This holds true not just for money but for any resource with a nonzero shadow price. For example, not having enough time for two activities (work and family) can create a situation in which you are unable to enjoy either, because of the moral tax on the time.

5. There is recent evidence favoring the notion that a zero price is special, that is, that there is hedonic discontinuity between a very small price and no price at all. Kristina Shampanier, Nina Mazar, and Dan Ariely, "Zero as a Special Price: The True Value of Free Products," *Marketing Science* 26, no. 6 (2007): 742–57.

6. The moral tax perspective is complementary to but distinct from transaction utility perspective, which has dominated consumer behavior research on price. Richard H. Thaler, "Toward a Positive Theory of Consumer Choice," *Journal of Economic Behavior & Organization* 1, no. 1 (1980): 39–60; "Mental Accounting and Consumer Choice," *Marketing Science* 4 (1985): 199–214; "Mental Accounting Matters," in *Choices, Values, and Frames*, edited by Daniel Kahneman and Amos Tversky (Cambridge University Press, 1999), pp. 241–68. Transaction utility refers to the pleasures of a good deal—a price lower than the standard or reference amount. Research on transaction utility typically explores the impact of framing, discounts, reference prices, and selling format variables.

7. See, for example, Drazen Prelec and George F. Loewenstein, "The Red and the Black: Mental Accounting of Savings and Debt," *Marketing Science* 17, no. 1 (1998): 4–28.

8. Ibid.

9. Eldar Shafir and Richard Thaler, "Invest Now, Drink Later, Spend Never: On the Mental Accounting of Delayed Consumption," *Journal of Economic Psychology* 27, no. 5 (2006): 694–712.

10. Dennis W. Rook, "The Buying Impulse," *Journal of Consumer Research* 14 (September 1987): 189–99; Dennis W. Rook and R. J. Fisher, "Normative Influence on Impulsive Buying Behavior," *Journal of Consumer Research* 22 (December 1995): 305–13.

11. A testimonial to the appeal of prepaid cards reads as follow: "We researched several motivation strategies and confirmed that prepaid cards are our single, most effective method to motivate behavior and ultimately drive sales." Ms. Karen Abene, Starz Entertainment, www.springbokservices.com/pdf/casestudies/Starz_Sales_Incentive_Program_Case_Study.pdf, p. 2.

12. Ran Kivetz and Itamar Simonson, "Self-Control for the Righteous: Toward a Theory of Precommitment to Indulgence," *Journal of Consumer Research* 29, no. 2 (September 2002): 199–217.

13. Prelec and Loewenstein, "The Red and the Black"; Dilip Soman and John T. Gourville, "Transaction Decoupling: How Price Bundling Affects the Decision to Consume," *Journal of Marketing Research* 38, no. 1 (2001): 30–45.

14. Prelec and Loewenstein, "The Red and the Black."

15. Ibid. Credit card bills share this unpleasant characteristic with other bills for things that are incidental to primary consumption, such as electricity, gas, insurance, or taxes.

16. See, for example, Nicole Jonker, "Payment Instruments as Perceived by Consumers: A Public Survey," DNB Working Paper 053 (De Nederlandsche Bank, 2005).

17. Elizabeth C. Hirschman, "Differences in Consumer Purchase Behavior by Credit Card Payment System," *Journal of Consumer Research* 6 (June 1979): 58–66.

18. Richard A. Feinberg, "Credit Cards as Spending Facilitating Stimuli: A Conditioning Explanation," *Journal of Consumer Research* 13, no. 3 (1986): 344–56; Drazen Prelec and Duncan Simester, "Always Leave Home Without It: A Further Investigation of the Credit-Card Effect on Willingness to Pay," *Marketing Letters* 12, no. 1 (2001): 5–12.

19. Prelec and Simester, "Always Leave Home Without It."

20. Ibid.

21. Dan Ariely, George F. Loewenstein, and Drazen Prelec, "'Coherent Arbitrariness': Stable Demand Curves without Stable Preferences," *Quarterly Journal of Economics* 118, no. 1 (2003): 73–105.

22. Jonathan Zinman, "Why Use Debit Instead of Credit? Consumer Choice in a Trillion Dollar Market," mimeo (Federal Reserve Bank of New York, 2005); Fusaro, "Debit vs. Credit."

23. Feinberg, "Credit Cards as Spending Facilitating Stimuli."

24. The considerations that make strong coupling unattractive to the buyer also make it attractive to the seller of services. This is nicely illustrated by a fake ad for a bogus product, "The Pocket-Penpoint," featured in the *California Lawyer* magazine. Targeting lawyers, consultants, and other time-rate professionals, the ad described a device that accommodated the client's credit card and charged the client's account in real time. Although it was obvious from the fine print that such a device did not exist, the ad still managed to elicit many purchase requests. "I thought the idea of having a client's money go instantly into your account was almost too good to be true," one potential customer remarked. The same characteristics that make the card attractive to the lawyer presumably make it painful to the client, which is why the device was described as being "topped with a handkerchief so it can be worn discreetly in a breast pocket." Prelec and Loewenstein, "The Red and the Black."

25. Samuel M. McClure, Jian Li, Damon Tomlin, Kim S. Cypert, Latané M. Montague, and P. Read Montague, "Neural Correlates of Behavioral Preference for Culturally Familiar Drinks," *Neuron* 44, no. 2 (2004): 379–87; Colin Camerer, George F. Loewenstein, and Drazen Prelec, "Neuroeconomics: How Neuroscience Can Inform Economics," *Journal of Economic Literature* 43 (March 2005): 9–64.

26. Brian Knutson, Scott Rick, G. Elliott Wimmer, Drazen Prelec, and George F. Loewenstein, "Neural Predictors of Purchases," *Neuron* 53 (January 2007): 147–56.

27. Ronit Bodner and Drazen Prelec, "Self-Signaling in a Neo-Calvinist Model of Everyday Decision Making," in *Psychology of Economic Decisions*, vol. 1, edited by Isabelle Brocas and Juan Carillo (Oxford University Press, 2003).

28. June P. Tangney, Roy F. Baumeister, and Angie Luzio Boone, "High Self-Control Predicts Good Adjustment, Less Pathology, Better Grades, and Interpersonal Success," *Journal of Personality* 72, no. 2 (2004): 271–324. Among the many psychological studies on self-control, the work generated by Walter Mischel's delay-of-gratification paradigm has been especially provocative in its implications. Mischel and his collaborators showed that the ability to delay gratification at age four or five assessed by how long a child could refrain from eating a small, immediately available piece of candy in expectation of getting a larger one later predicted performance and well-being in high school and beyond, on a variety of measures. Apparently, the skills that allow a child to avoid temptation in a relatively inconsequential laboratory choice task may also be those critical to success and adaptation in future life. Walter Mischel, Yuichi Shoda, and Monica L. Rodriguez, "Delay of Gratification in Children," *Science* 244, no. 4907 (May 1989): 933–38.

29. Baba Shiv and Alexander Fedorikhin, "Heart and Mind in Conflict: The Interplay of Affect and Cognition in Consumer Decision Making," *Journal of Consumer Research* 26, no. 3 (December 1999): 278–92; Mark Muraven and Roy F. Baumeister, "Self-Regulation and Depletion of Limited Resources: Does Self-Control Resemble a Muscle?" *Psychological Bulletin* 126, no. 2 (2000): 247–59.

30. George Ainslie, "Specious Reward–Behavioral Theory of Impulsiveness and Impulse Control," *Psychological Bulletin* 82, no. 4 (1975): 463–96.

31. Kathleen D. Vohs and Ronald J. Faber, "Spent Resources? Self-Regulatory Resource Availability Affects Impulse Buying," *Journal of Consumer Research* 33 (March 2007): 537–47.

32. Shane Frederick, Nathan Novemsky, Jing Wang, Ravi Dhar, and Stephen Nowlis, "Neglect of Opportunity Costs in Consumer Choice," Working Paper (Cambridge, Mass.: Massachusetts Institute of Technology, 2006).

33. George F. Loewenstein and Ted O'Donoghue, "'We Can Do This the Easy Way or the Hard Way': Negative Emotions, Self-Regulation and the Law," *University of Chicago Law Review* 73 (Winter 2006): 183–206.

34. Scott Rick, Cynthia Cryder, and George F. Loewenstein, "Tightwads and Spendthrifts," *Journal of Consumer Research* 34 (June 2007): 767–82.

35. Prelec and Loewenstein, "The Red and the Black."

36. Echoes of this vision can be detected in the new freeconomics movement. See "Freeconomics," Economist.com, web-only premium content, November 15,

2007 (www.economist.com/theWorldIn/business/displayStory.cfm?story_id= 10094757andd=2008). A key advocate is Chris Anderson, editor-in-chief at *Wired Magazine*; his book *The Long Tale: The Rise of Freeconomics*, is scheduled for publication in 2009.

37. James J. Choi, David Laibson, Brigitte C. Madrian, and Andrew Metrick, "Optimal Defaults," *American Economic Review Papers and Proceedings* 93 (2003): 180–85; Richard H. Thaler and Cass R. Sunstein, *Nudge: Improving Decisions about Health, Wealth, and Happiness* (Yale University Press 2008).

38. Richard H. Thaler and Shlomo Benartzi, "Save More Tomorrow: Using Behavioral Economics to Increase Employee Savings," *Journal of Political Economy* 112 (2004): 164–87.

39. Self-reported data on attitudes to payment and consumption support the existence of such a smug segment. George Loewenstein, Drazen Prelec, and Roberto Weber, "What, Me Worry? A Psychological Perspective on Economic Aspects of Retirement," in *Psychological Perspectives on Retirement*, edited by Henry J. Aaron (Brookings Institution and Russell Sage Foundation, 2000).

KENNETH CHENAULT

5

The Future of Consumer Payments: An Insider's Perspective

The payments industry that I know is both global and dynamic. It is without a doubt a highly competitive industry, one that is rapidly innovating and evolving. It is an industry that exists in various stages, largely depending on geography. In some markets customer needs are simple. Products are basic and providers are few. In other countries customer demands are greater. Products are high tech and the competitive landscape is quite diverse. But regardless of its evolutionary stage in any given market, the purpose of the industry remains the same: to facilitate the conduct of commerce and improve the efficiency of day-to-day transactions among consumers and businesses.

As we all know, the global environment is evolving at an accelerated pace, not just for payments but for all businesses. So even though I know my industry well, I also know that to attempt to predict the future of payments is an assignment fraught with peril. But while I can't predict the future with certainty, I can offer my perspective on trends that are currently under way across the industry, trends that will likely shape the evolution of payments over the short, medium, and long term.

Before I look ahead, however, I want to first take a moment to look back—specifically, to look back to how American Express became a payment company. While I'm always on the lookout for opportunities to showcase our employees and our company, let me assure you this history lesson is not intended to be self-serving. It is relevant to today's topic because I believe American Express's own history offers insight into how the overall industry has evolved and how, even today, it continues to reinvent itself to meet, or anticipate, the needs of customers.

Our founders include two names that are familiar throughout the business world: Henry Wells and William Fargo. In 1850 we opened our doors as an express company, a freight company. We moved packages and currency for people across states and across territories. Think Federal Express with stagecoaches and that was us.

As the United States expanded during the latter half of the nineteenth century, so did the needs of our customers. American goods and materials were not just being shipped between states, but to the rest of the world as well. In response, we expanded our own corporate geography, setting up freight offices in a number of international capitals. As the country prospered, more and more Americans wanted to see the world, so we formed a travel agency to help them go overseas. International journeys, whether for cargo or people, also had to be paid for. At this point in history there was no means of payment that could easily cross borders, so we created our own, inventing both the American Express travelers cheque and the money order.

By the 1950s customers demanded greater financial flexibility, both at home and while traveling. To meet this need we launched our first charge card in 1958. And this year, we're proud to celebrate its fiftieth anniversary.

As a former history major, I always look for ways to learn from the past. And while I've gained many insights by studying my company's 158-year history, two insights are particularly relevant for today's conversation.

The first is the importance of driving change, not only in your own company but also through your industry. American Express has shown the flexibility and resolve to reinvent itself, adapting to customer needs and to a changing marketplace. Given the dramatic pace of change across the industry today, this capability is clearly an important asset for any payment company to have.

My second takeaway is that, at its core, the payments business is dependent on a very basic element—trust. Trust that your payment will be correctly handled. Trust that your interests and assets will be protected. Trust that someone will be there when you need help. Whether it is shipping gold from New York to San Francisco, having a merchant accept a travelers cheque half a world away, or using a credit card to make an online purchase, the payments business is clearly a trust business.

I will acknowledge, upfront, that confidence in the payments industry has eroded over the last couple of years. The credit card industry in particular has fallen short of the mark in some of its practices, and any assessment of the future of payments must recognize this. The Federal Reserve Bank and other regulators are working to address specific card practices, and as I'll discuss later on, I recognize and support their hard work in striking an appropriate balance to protect consumers without curtailing the innovation and competition that exist across the industry.

Before discussing some of the trends currently under way across payments, let me first offer some basics on the industry. The term *payments* may sound simple, but it actually covers a lot of ground. The industry today offers extensive choice. Payment transactions can involve a number of parties and take a number of forms, ranging from simple to complex.

For a basic transaction between a buyer and a seller, customers can choose to pay now, pay later, or pay in advance. Within each category there are then many choices of product. For example, if buyers wish to pay at the point of sale, they can use cash, which involves only the buyer and the seller. Or they can pay by check, which typically involves five parties: the customer, his or her bank, the seller, the seller's bank, and the Federal Reserve. Or they can use a debit card, which involves a seller, a buyer, their banks, a debit network, and potentially a processor or two.

Given the broad array of choice in a typical developed market, it can be hard to keep track of what the term *payments* actually includes, so figure 5-1 displays basic product definitions, depending on whether a payment is made now, later, or in advance, and covers everything

Figure 5-1. *Payment Industry Definitions*

Pay later	
Credit/charge	Card indicating that the holder has been granted a line of credit. With it, the holder can make purchases and/or withdraw cash up to a prearranged ceiling.
Pay now	
Debit	Card that enables the holder to have his or her purchases directly deducted from funds at a deposit-taking institution.
ACH/wire	Electronic payments network that allows funds to be electronically debited or credited to a checking account, savings account, financial institution general ledger account, or credited to a loan account.
Money transfer	Funds transmitted electronically between consumers or businesses, where the funds are retrieved at money transferring agent location or deposited directly into a deposit account.
Cash	Currency and coins
Check	Written order from one party to another requiring the payer to pay a specified sum on demand to the payee or to a third party specified by the payer.
Pay in advance	
Prepaid	Instrument on which value is stored and for which the holder has paid the issuer in advance.

Source: American Express Company.

from wire transfers to credit cards. Payment users have a range of options.

Over the past few years, I've also added an overlay to this list, that of emerging payments, which can cover all types of transactions. Payment companies, such as my own, along with other providers and technology companies, are developing new products and access devices that rethink traditional formulas. Online products, mobile devices, and contactless payments—to name just a few—are responding to, or oftentimes leading, customer demand. In many cases these innovations are improving the ease and efficiency of customer transactions, and they clearly have the potential to significantly impact the industry. Another basic fact about payments is the diversity of its participants. There are many players across the industry, from large companies, providing multiple products and services, to specialty processors who perform a single function. In some cases, including the customer and the merchant, up to seven different participants or companies may touch a single payment transaction. Payment transactions are sliced and diced among many companies and processors. Some have a niche within a specific area of processing and look specifically to expand their volumes and scale. Others focus on the end user, offering value and services to the payment customer—be it a consumer or a business.

Looking across this landscape, American Express and Discover are the only providers that have a material presence across multiple pieces of any payment chain. Both companies issue products, acquire merchants, process transactions, and operate networks. In the American Express business model, for example, the objective is to serve high-spending, affluent card members, providing them with premium value such as through rewards or unique merchant offers. At the same time, however, the company looks to improve its operating efficiencies by attracting more card holders, merchants, and spending. Being an issuer, acquirer, and processor gives American Express the flexibility and means to invest in and implement a wider range of innovations and therefore meet a wider range of customer needs.

This is, of course, just a snapshot of the industry today. Over time, new competitors will certainly join the marketplace, particularly in the emerging areas noted earlier. Already companies such as Verizon, BillMeLater, and PayPal are adding innovations and options to the industry and for customers. Given the global growth under way across payments, there is clearly room for new approaches, and I expect new providers, technologies, and geographies will further expand the marketplace. Beyond new entrants, we are likely to see more partnering across the industry. Participants will partner with each other to develop new features and technologies that can provide customized services with maximum efficiency.

Some people may not view payments as a growth industry. Announcements have come from some of my American peers that they are diversifying into other product lines because they consider the U.S. credit card industry to be mature. That's one view, but I believe it is a narrow view. It only considers one payment product within a range of product options; it only considers one market across a vast global map.

I hold a different view. I believe the payments industry as a whole offers a tremendous amount of long-term potential for reasons that fall into three categories: product penetration, technology, and geography. There's not always a clean break across these growth drivers, but some examples follow.

The first driver of growth is product penetration. Even within a developed economy such as the United States, electronic payment products still have a lot of unused runway. Among American consumers, it is estimated that cash and checks still account for more than 55 percent of spending. For small and mid-size businesses in the United States that number is 85 percent. This translates into two business opportunities. For a product provider like American Express, it means the chance for increased volumes, particularly as specific industries such as health care and raw materials move to accept plastic. For the financial system as a whole, it means the opportunity to further improve processing efficiencies and drive down costs by taking even more paper out of the pipeline.

The second trend that will drive growth in electronic payments is technology, the most significant example of which is the Internet. For years futurists have been talking about the inevitability of a cashless society, one where a swipe or a tap will buy you a newspaper or a morning bagel. The payments industry as a whole is clearly making strides in this direction. But consumers are not concerned with meeting predictions, and as a significant number of product pilots have shown over the last few years, they remain committed to cash for certain purchases. Just as the futurists of fifty years ago thought we would all be in flying cars by now, a cashless society is another prediction that seems to be falling by the wayside.

The exception to this is the one truly cashless society that exists today—and that is the virtual world. Cash and checks are essentially nonplayers when it comes to the Internet, so anyone conducting business online is automatically driving the growth of electronic payments.

Online commerce will continue to grow robustly over the next five years, albeit at a somewhat slower rate than the adoption years of the late 1990s. And this growth in online spending will clearly drive growth in payments. In 2007 U.S. retail consumers spent $150 billion online, a large number, but still a small proportion of their total spending of $4 trillion. But, while cash and checks still account for a majority of consumer offline spending, as noted before, online spending is 100 percent electronic. With online purchases expected to grow at a compounded rate of 19 percent between now and 2012, the opportunities for payment providers will expand significantly.

This sizable business opportunity is attracting a significant number of new players into the field, with retailers themselves, real-time credit products, and companies such as PayPal joining traditional credit and debit providers. This competition is bringing innovation, efficiency, and growth into the payments marketplace, something we all benefit from.

The third trend that will drive the growth of payments over the medium and long term is geography.

While certain developed economies have been using some form of electronic payments for years, a number of significant economies continue to be primarily cashcentric. Among this group are the BRIC countries (Brazil, Russia, India, and China), which offer the broad opportunity of high economic growth, along with specific opportunities in payments.

Economies evolve differently as they develop, and that will no doubt be true for a number of these cashcentric markets. For example, new technologies may make it possible for countries such as China or India to skip the steps taken by Western economies. Instead of progressively moving from cash to checks to plastic, advances in wireless telecom may allow them to vault past the need for a physical card or check and go straight to an electronic account number. But while their devices and means of access may differ from other markets, I believe their overall development will follow a consistent trend. Even allowing for differences in culture and technology, this trend is quite clear. It has consistently been seen that as per capita GDP increases within a country, the number of electronic payments rises substantially. As a country's educational levels rise, as personal income grows, as technology becomes more broadly available, the use of electronic payments expands, all of which highlights the growth potential of the markets in countries such as China, India, and Indonesia.

As a payment provider I look at the size and scope of this opportunity and want to attack it immediately, but then quickly recognize that income growth alone will not be sufficient to drive growth in payments. As noted, the payments business is not just about transactional capabilities. It also depends on trust.

Businesses and consumers are not going to generate the level of growth implied here without trust. And not just trust in payment providers such as American Express, but also in a wide array of people and institutions including taxing authorities, the banking system, the currency market, and regulators.

Moving away from a cash-based economy requires a basic level of government and corporate infrastructure. It requires a popular belief in the equity of national policies and their fair implementation. Without these basics in an economy, even the most innovative payment product will have trouble competing with the proverbial cash under the mattress.

But more important than the impact on the payments industry is the greater impact on the country itself. Without trust in the basics, economies can be hampered, the potential of a society will be limited, and individual growth and productivity can be restrained. This trust is essential. It is a prerequisite to generating and sustaining any degree of long-term economic growth.

As someone who heads a large global payments company, I spend a lot of my time on technology investments, processing costs, and telecom capabilities. But one of my more significant roles is to be a steward of the American Express brand. Given its long history, American Express has a unique legacy to uphold. A legacy of service, of quality, of integrity. As a result the company places a great deal of importance on this fundamental idea of trust. My view is that while the global payments system must be open and flexible enough to allow for many different players, it must always be based on integrity and trust.

Payment providers, therefore, must be accountable for living up to high standards. Providers who undermine trust clearly limit their own growth potential. For example, I do not believe a company has much of a future if it earns the majority of its revenues when customers make a mistake or do not conform to a rule. "Gotcha" pricing is not the way to build a sustainable business model or to maintain long-term customer relationships and trust. I believe a company's long-term health is only assured when customers receive value for their money and feel they are treated well.

While American Express does take action when a customer fails to pay an account on time or bounces a check, certain practices don't make the cut. One example is "universal default." This is the practice of raising the interest rate for a customer on your own product because he or she is delinquent in paying someone else. That customer remains current with you, but the customer's rate gets raised because of problems with another lender. A number of companies adopted this practice and generated higher short-term revenues as a result. American Express made a conscious choice several years ago not to implement this practice across its card base. It just did not feel right.

The credit card industry has been criticized for universal default and a number of other practices, and industry representatives must respond to these criticisms in order to restore the trust necessary for a healthy marketplace that can foster innovation and long-term growth.

Government plays a critical role in bolstering public confidence by maintaining a reliable and balanced regulatory framework. As industries change and evolve, so must this framework. An example is the work currently under way at the Federal Reserve and other regulators to update rules governing the credit card industry and to strengthen consumer protections. We may not agree with all of the proposals being considered by the Fed, but we do recognize why these actions are being taken, and we support the efforts.

The new rules being proposed by regulators are sweeping and will mark the most important regulatory change for the credit card industry in at least twenty-five years. It is our hope that these changes will bolster trust—trust in the regulatory system and trust between consumers and payment providers. We believe regulators recognize the need for balanced action and the industry's concerns about unintended consequences. We believe the Fed will be open to industry comments and that the final guidelines will protect consumer interests while at the same time supporting appropriate access to credit within a competitive marketplace.

Our mutual goal needs to be to stop the abuses that exist today, to strengthen consumer confidence, and to do so without impeding the growth and development of innovation, choice, and value that will benefit customers in the future. I believe the payments industry is at a very exciting point in its evolution. It is a journey that has been characterized by ongoing innovation, heated competition, and high customer expectations.

The industry also has enormous breadth, because it is not a pure stand-alone business. Yes, it has its own products and issues, but at the same time it is embedded into multiple industries, across multiple markets, and used by multiple customers for almost every type of current commercial transaction. This breadth and diversity have attracted vast numbers of providers ranging from large global companies to local banks and credit unions. Trillions of dollars, euros, yen, and RMB get transferred and settled each year. Across the industry, payment systems operate with exceptional efficiency and provide strong value to customers. Some providers offer low cost and large scale. Others offer high value and service. Some, like my own company, are combinations of both.

Given this range of products and providers, I believe it is a misnomer to call the payments industry a commodity business. The term *commodity* implies a sameness that just does not exist. It implies mass production and low value added. The global payment system that exists today is far from a commodity. It is a facilitator of global commerce. It is a driver of business growth. It is a means of developing national economies on behalf of all citizens. For all these reasons I believe payment systems should be viewed as economic assets, not as utilities.

To ensure future growth and continued innovation, the industry should remain open and not be restricted by inappropriate barriers. Regulation will occur, but the regulatory approach to payments should be one that sustains trust, while at the same time encouraging productive, value-added growth on behalf of customers. This industry clearly has a great deal of untapped potential, and the realization of that potential is a challenge to look forward to.

NICHOLAS ECONOMIDES

6

Competition Policy Issues in the Consumer Payments Industry

At the completion of a sale, money changes hands. Money changing hands could be in cash or checks, and, for the last few decades, also be in electronically transmitted funds or a guarantee of prompt electronic payment to the merchant. Such electronic payments could come from a company that provides credit to customers (such as a bank organized under the Visa or MasterCard trade names[1]), from one that facilitates transactions but typically does not provide credit (such as American Express), or directly from the bank where the customer has demand deposits.[2] The payment system intermediary facilitates the payment to the merchant by guaranteeing that the merchant receives the money, and at the same time can also offer a variety of services to the cardholder, ranging from credit services to frequent flyer miles.

Credit and other bank cards facilitate transactions between merchants and consumers. Card networks collect significant fees from merchants to facilitate those transactions.[3] The market for facilitation is dominated by the Visa and MasterCard networks. Visa had a 42 percent share of the U.S. credit card market in 2007, MasterCard 29 percent, American Express 24 percent, and Discover 5 percent.[4]

I thank Bob Litan and participants in the Future of Consumer Payments Conference at the Brookings Institution.

113

Both Visa and MasterCard charge fees (primarily to merchants) that are significantly above costs—some report that total card costs are only 13 to 15 percent of the fees charged and that total fees are about $30 to $48 billion per year.[5] This combination of fees that are significantly above cost and high market shares suggests that current fees reflect market power.[6]

Setups of Three- and Four-Party Card Networks

The intermediation of American Express involves three parties, the cardholder, the merchant, and American Express, hence the name three-party card network. The basic structure of this setup is presented in figure 6-1. It is important that the network (American Express) can charge fees on both sides of the market, or can charge only one side and subsidize the other. This two-sidedness is a fundamental feature of network structure and can be exploited to support high transaction fees.

In a multiparty credit card association, such as Visa or MasterCard, merchants deal directly with acquiring banks that intermediate transactions to issuing banks that issue cards to consumers and ultimately send them bills as well. A transaction between a customer and a merchant conducted through Visa or MasterCard is intermediated by both the acquiring bank and the issuing bank. Figure 6-2 shows the intermediation in a Visa or MasterCard network where the functions of acquiring (a merchant) and issuing (a card to a customer) can be handled by different banks. Thus, in this setup we have four parties: the merchant, the acquiring bank, the issuing bank, and the cardholder.[7] The two-sidedness remains important in more complex networks such as those of MasterCard and Visa.

In four-party networks, such as MasterCard and Visa, three markets are connected in sequence in each transaction, and the surplus of each end-to-end transaction is divided among the markets (figure 6-3). The three markets are between the issuer and the consumer (market 1), between the acquirer and the issuer (market 2), and between the merchant and the acquirer (market 3).

Figure 6-1. *A Three-Party Card Network*

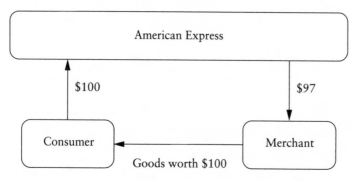

The interchange fee is the amount an acquiring bank pays an issuing bank when a merchant accepts a Visa or MasterCard for a purchase, that is, the fee that changes hands in market 2. The acquiring bank pays the merchant the amount of the transaction less both the interchange fee and an additional fee that the acquiring bank keeps for itself. Visa and MasterCard set maximum interchange fees, and almost no banks deviate from them.[8] Interchange fees in the United States are approximately 1.8 percent on average.[9] The transaction fees the merchants pay are at

Figure 6-2. *A Four-Party Card Network*

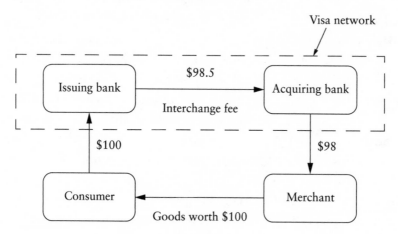

Figure 6-3. *Three Sequential Markets in Four-Party Network*

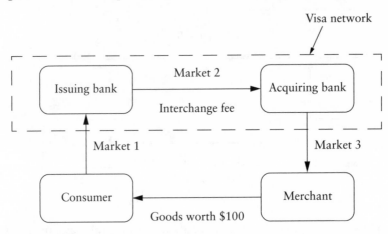

least as high as the interchange fees. Even if the market between acquirers and merchants were perfectly competitive, acquirers would have to charge merchants at least as much as the interchange fee because the interchange fee is their marginal cost (which they of course need to pay). Most commentators agree that the market between the acquirers and the merchants (market 3) is effectively competitive. Thus, if there is market power in the four-party network, it has to be in markets 1 and 2, although its final effects manifest in market 3 as well.

Both issuing and acquiring banks can charge (or be charged) on both sides of the market they intermediate.[10] That is, decisions affecting pricing on one side of the market will have consequences on the other side. For example, a decision by Visa or MasterCard, the issuing banks themselves, or regulators to reduce the fees that merchants pay may either increase the fees customers pay for the card or may reduce awards or other incentives that issuing banks offer to customers. The extent to which this will occur depends on whether the issuers are passing to their customers the (interchange) fees they receive from the merchants through the acquiring banks. That is, it depends on how competitive the card issuing market is. Of course, consumers will likely benefit when a merchant reduces prices to reflect lower intermediation fees. Because of the complexity of the market structure and the varying degrees of market power in the three markets identified, policy recommendations need to be carefully examined in terms of their impact on all sides of the markets.

How Card Networks Keep Transaction Facilitation Fees High

The card networks impose various contractual restrictions, such as those against surcharges, steering, and discrimination, as well as, until recently, one to honor all cards, which collectively prohibits or discourages merchants from favoring cards that offer better terms. This both reduces competition among card networks in getting merchants' business and supports high interchange fees. These restrictions are critical.

Credit card networks have high price-to-cost markups despite non-dominant market shares. There is evidence of very significant markups of price above cost, with total costs representing only 15 percent of revenue. It is highly unlikely that consumers receive from card networks anything approaching the fee level charged to merchants. The implied profit rates are comparable to those of Microsoft and Intel, which each have a dominant and almost monopoly market share. So the interesting question is how Visa with a 42 percent market share and MasterCard with a 29 percent share achieve such high markups and market power. An answer will also suggest ways in which distortions can be reduced in the market for transaction facilitation.

If confronted with the cost of their transactions, consumers would most likely use the card with the lowest fee in businesses where multiple cards are accepted. Of course, price is only one of a number of consumer considerations. Everything else equal, however, consumers are more likely to use cards that impose lower direct costs to them. So, if consumers faced directly the costs of intermediation for their transactions, they would choose to use lower-cost cards. Competition among the card networks would therefore drive fees down.

The networks use a multipronged strategy to achieve an equilibrium with less competition. The first part of their strategy is to ensure that a cardholder does not directly face the cost of using a particular card for payment. This requires two conditions, that the consumer not pay more to the issuer for a card that has higher costs, and that the consumer not pay more to the merchant when using a card that has higher costs. The two-sidedness of the card network can easily ensure the first condition because costs can be recovered from the merchant side. The second condition is more complicated to implement.

Focusing on the first condition, we note that cardholders do not need to face the merchant's cost of their transactions because of the two-sidedness of the network. As long as the network can collect from one side (the merchants), it does not need to collect from the other (the cardholders), and can in fact even subsidize the cardholders. Therefore, unless the merchants impose additional costs on the cardholders when the network imposes such costs on the merchants, the cardholders will not face transaction costs directly and therefore will not in general use the lowest-cost card.

Second, by imposing contractual obligations on merchants, networks make certain that merchants cannot charge different prices (to reflect the different card fees) for the same item to consumers who use different cards.

Card networks have used a number of instruments to make it difficult for merchants to respond to card fee differences. This of course facilitates high fees. The first such instrument is the no-surcharge rule, a contractual restriction imposed on merchants. The second was the honor-all-cards rule, which was abolished in 2003 after an antitrust suit by the merchants.[11]

The No-Surcharge, No-Discrimination, and Most-Favored-Customer Rules

Essentially the no-surcharge rule says that a merchant can charge the same amount for a Visa transaction as for cash, but if a merchant offers a discount for cash payments, he cannot offer the same discount to a comparable card (MasterCard). Additionally, if a merchant offers a discount to a comparable card, he must offer it to Visa as well.[12] This, in economics, is called a most-favored-customer rule. The effect of the no-surcharge rule is that the merchant cannot offer better terms to customers who buy with MasterCard than with Visa, although it would make sense to do so if MasterCard's fees to the merchant were lower. This rule allows no price flexibility in the merchant's pricing. It is as if Coca-Cola were to impose the requirement that a can of Pepsi be sold at the same price as a can of Coke. The only option for the merchant who does not like the fees of a particular network is to not accept that network's card. An additional restriction is the no-discrimination rule, which MasterCard phrases this way: "Merchants may not engage in acceptance practices or procedures that discriminate against, or discourage the use of, MasterCard cards in favor of any other card brand."[13]

Industrial organization theory has established that most-favored-customer rules can be used to increase prices to collusive levels.[14] The intuition for this result is simple. Most-favored-customer rules impose on a merchant the requirement to cut prices to all customers with whom it has agreed on this rule if it cuts the price to any one customer. Thus the loss of revenue implied by a price cut to one customer is multiplied in the presence of the most-favored-customer rule. It follows that a firm is less likely to decrease a price under the most-favored-customer rule. This effect is strengthened when a number of firms put these rules into effect.

The Honor-All-Cards Rule

High merchant fees were threatened by technological change. Debit networks, typically with PIN verification, offered lower merchant fees than traditional card networks. Debit cards in the MasterCard and Visa networks also offered much lower fees than signature-based cards. To avoid loss of profits in credit cards, the networks imposed an honor-all-cards rule. This required that if a merchant accepted one Visa card, he had to accept all Visa cards, both credit and debit, issued by any bank in the Visa network.

There were two aspects of this rule. First, if a merchant accepted a certain type of card (say, Visa debit) issued by one bank (say, Citibank), he was required to accept the same type of card (in this case, Visa debit) issued by another bank. The rule also imposed the requirement that a merchant accept any other Visa products (such as Visa credit cards) if he accepted one (such as a Visa debit card). Visa's rules stated that "the Merchant shall promptly honor all valid Visa cards when properly presented as payment."

The second requirement, that is, to accept different types of cards of the same brand, was essentially tying and has anticompetitive consequences. To put this in context, it would be anticompetitive were Microsoft to say, "If your corporation buys Windows, it must also buy MS Office," or were Dell to say, "If you buy Dell servers you must also buy Dell laptops."

The honor-all-cards rule is now illegal in the United States, merchants having won an antitrust suit against the card networks in 2003. The court essentially forbade the second requirement but confirmed the first—that networks can require merchants to honor all cards across all member banks for a specific type of card (such as a debit card).

Effects of the Present Equilibrium

Transaction facilitation fees charged to merchants, driven primarily by the interchange fee, are significantly above the total cost of facilitating transactions. Because most merchants do not offer discounts for paying in cash, those who primarily do use cash end up paying, through higher product prices, for the costs of card use, which for the most part is by more wealthy consumers. Card transactions are subsidized by cash transactions. Cardholders do not see the fees imposed on merchants, only retail product prices, which increase for all consumers. Additionally, as the networks try to expand by signing up more issuing bank members, they have incentives to increase their interchange fees to make entry into their network more attractive and to avoid exit.[15] As acquirers "typically 'blend' their pricing and charge each merchant one overall merchant service fee based on the projected proportionate volume of cards from each scheme"[16] (network), "in effect, the lower cost scheme therefore subsidizes the higher cost scheme with the merchant receiving only perhaps some marginal benefit of the lower cost scheme's interchange rates."[17] Thus, at the present equilibrium, high-cost card transactions are subsidized by low-cost transactions. And, under the present rules, interbrand (internetwork) competition does not produce lower fees—quite the opposite.[18]

Improving Efficiency

How can efficiency be improved in this sector? The optimal approach is to help the markets work. Recognizing that the credit card setup comprises three sequential two-sided markets, as described, we need to consider how to improve and enhance competition on the merchant side (between merchants and acquiring banks), between issuing and acquiring banks, and on the consumer side (between consumers and issuing banks).

Changes between Merchants and Acquiring Banks (Market 3)

On the merchant side, I propose that card contracts allow for merchant flexibility in acceptance and pricing depending on the card's brand and type as well as on the fees charged to the merchant. That is, a merchant should be allowed to offer different discounts (or surcharges) to consumers for using a particular card if that card offers the merchant lower (or higher) fees. This requires, of course, that the no-surcharge and no-discrimination rules be eliminated from the contracts.[19]

The direct consequence of changing these rules will allow the merchants to make customers face the costs of transaction facilitation, which will increase internetwork and intranetwork competition. First, the change in the rules will increase competition between the products of the same network, resulting in lower fees for all of these products. A customer faced with, say, a lower fee when using a Visa debit card rather than a Visa signature card will use Visa debit. Second, the change in the rules will increase competition between the card networks and thus lower fees across the board. A customer faced, say, with a lower fee from MasterCard than Visa will use MasterCard.

Changes between Issuing and Acquiring Banks (Market 2)

The network, not the market, now sets the maximum interchange fee between issuing and acquiring banks and practically no bank in the network deviates from it. The interchange fee is set high, leading acquirers to charge merchants an even higher fee. Card networks have built-in incentives to increase the interchange fee to attract more issuers.

To reduce the interchange fee, I propose that the network no longer set the maximum interchange fee. Let it instead be determined in bilateral negotiations between an issuer and an acquirer, starting from a zero fee basis (par). This would allow for bilateral negotiations between the banks that could result in a variety of interchange fees depending on the specific pair of issuer and acquirer and their competitive conditions. The system could start from a default zero interchange fee, with the market determining any positive or negative adjustment of the fee in a bank pair.

There are two objections to this scenario. The first is that it might lead to too many bilateral contracts. But there is significant concentration among acquirers, with 86 percent of all Visa and MasterCard volume generated by the top ten acquiring banks. Similarly, 84 percent of this volume is generated by the top ten issuers. Therefore ninety contracts generate 72 percent of all MasterCard and Visa volume.[20] The second objection is that an issuer can hold out for a high (monopoly) fee to an acquirer. To the extent that this is a unilateral exercise of monopoly power that was acquired legitimately, it should not be an antitrust concern. High fees by a particular issuer who brings high value transactions will hopefully attract competition by other issuers for the same customers and will, in the long run, have these customers signed by a different issuer, resulting in lower fees because of competition among issuers. Additionally, it is not clear that the imposition of high fees is not happening right now with the network setting the monopoly fee for all issuers. With bilateral negotiations, the high fees will be limited to a few issuers instead. Moreover, since the fee will not be set collectively by the network, the incentive to set a high fee across the board to attract more issuers to the network will be eliminated.

Consequences of the Changes in the Rules

Allowing interbrand competition is expected to increase competition between the card networks. It is difficult to estimate the extent of additional competition and the extent of the reduction in fees. The "natural experiment" of Australia might give us some insight.[21] In 2003, the Reserve Bank of Australia (RBA) reduced interchange fees for credit cards in Australia from an average of 0.95 to 0.55 percent, and in November 2006 to 0.50 percent, and at the same time allowed merchants to impose surcharges.[22] Even though surcharging was not widespread, merchant fees fell even more than the interchange fees. The Reserve Bank of Australia made the following observation in its annual report:

> The fall in the average merchant service fee since the reforms is significantly larger than the decline in the average interchange fee. . . . These lower merchant costs are feeding through into lower prices for goods and services (or smaller price increases than otherwise would have occurred). While merchants would undoubtedly have hoped that these lower costs translated into increased profits, competition means that just as the banks passed on their lower costs to merchants, so too must merchants pass on their lower costs to consumers.[23]

Additionally, the overall cost to the economy of facilitating transactions fell.[24] The reforms outlined are likely to cause significantly lower fees for facilitating transactions. The subsidy from cash transactions to credit transactions is likely to be reduced. This will help less affluent customers, who tend to pay in cash. Within credit card transactions, the subsidy from high fee cards to low fee cards will be reduced.

Conclusion

Card network fees are considerably higher than card network costs. This is facilitated by rules imposed on the merchants that do not allow merchants to steer consumers to cards that carry lower fees. The no-surcharge and no-discrimination rules force merchants to not charge different prices to customers using different cards even though merchants may pay different fees to the card networks. Abolition of these rules would help merchants impose the cost of the payment option they use on consumers. Abolition of these rules will increase competition in payment systems, both across card networks and within each card network.

Notes

1. For many years Visa and MasterCard functioned as not-for-profit associations of member banks. They recently made initial public stock offerings.

2. Although credit and noncredit cards started as single-store cards or single-product cards (such as travel services), they quickly evolved into payment systems used for a large variety of transactions.

3. Consumers pay extra for credit.

4. This is reported in the May 2008 issue of the *Nilson Report*, a trade publication, on credit card networks, and based on credit card purchase volume, excluding both cash volume, such as advances, and debit cards. Similarly, in 2006 the market shares were almost identical: Visa 42 percent, MasterCard 29 percent, American Express 23 percent, and Discover 5 percent. Discover Financial Services was spun off by Morgan Stanley in 2007. In the U.S. debit card market that year, market shares were Visa 48 percent and MasterCard 14 percent. See also Associated Press, "How Visa Operates," Forbes.com, February 25, 2008 (www.forbes.com/markets/feeds/afx/2008/02/25/afx4694434.html).

5. See "Interchange fee," Wikipedia, February 21, 2009 (http://en.wikipedia.org/wiki/Interchange_fee), and "NRF Welcomes Senate Bill Requiring Visa and MasterCard to Negotiate over Hidden Annual Fee," National Retail Federation, June 5, 2008 (www.nrf.com/modules.php?name=News&op=viewlive&sp_id=530). These are fees and costs solely for transaction facilitation, not those in the credit market in which many card networks also participate.

6. That American Express has charged higher merchant fees than Visa or MasterCard likely reflects the higher income of its customers, additional services American Express offers, and the fact that until recently it did not offer credit and therefore did not make money on credit. Higher American Express fees therefore do not mean that Visa's and MasterCard's fees are or might be competitive. In any event, lower Visa and MasterCard fees would likely create competitive pressure on American Express to lower its fees.

7. In a three-party setup, such as American Express and Diners Club, a single bank handles both the acquiring and the issuing functions. American Express

now also has a four-party network, in which it is the single acquiring bank, after the restriction by the MasterCard and Visa networks prohibiting member banks from issuing American Express cards was ruled anticompetitive in *United States v. Visa U.S.A.* 344 F.3d 229.

8. Visa's current interchange fees are available at its U.S. website (http://usa. visa.com/download/merchants/visa-usa-interchange-rates.pdf).

9. See "Visa Hikes Overall Interchange 0.6%, Effective April 14," *Digital-TransactionsNews*, April 12, 2007 (www.digitaltransactions.net/newsstory.cfm? newsid=1311).

10. Similarly, in the three-party setup of American Express and Diners Club, the network can charge on both sides, that is, the merchants as well as the customers.

11. See "Settled Merchant Lawsuit," MasterCardWorldwide (www.mastercard. com/us/company/en/newsroom/merch_law.html [March 3, 2009]).

12. See *Card Acceptance and Chargeback Management Guidelines for Visa Merchants* (San Francisco: Visa U.S.A., 2008), p. 10 (http://usa.visa.com/download/ merchants/card_acceptance_guide.pdf): "No Surcharging. Always treat Visa transactions like any other transaction; that is, you may not impose any surcharge on a Visa transaction. You may, however, offer a discount for cash or another form of payment (such as a proprietary card or gift certificate) provided that the offer is clearly disclosed to customers and the cash price is presented as a discount from the standard price charged for all other forms of payment. The discount may not be applied to [a] 'comparable card.' A 'comparable card' is any other branded, general purpose payment card that uses the cardholder's signature as the primary means of cardholder authorization (e.g., MasterCard, Discover, American Express). Any discount made available to cardholders who pay with 'comparable cards' must also be made available to cardholders who wish to pay with Visa cards."

13. See Lloyd Constantine, Gorden Schnell, Reiko Cyrs, and Michelle Peters, "The VISA Check/MasterMoney Antitrust Litigation," Constantine Cannon LLP, 2006, p. 24 (www.constantinecannon.com/pdf_etc/THEVISACHECKMASTER MONEYANTITRUSTLITIGATION.pdf).

14. See Steven C. Salop, "Practices That (Credibly) Facilitate Oligopoly Coordination," in *New Developments in the Analysis of Market Structure*, edited by Joseph E. Stiglitz and G. Frank Mathewson (New York: Macmillan 1986).

15. See, for example, Pete Hisey, "How High Can You Go?" *Credit Card Management* (April 1999): 105: "Visa, which says it has been at a disadvantage to MasterCard in the amount of cash it can allow an issuer to earn, says that its increases in interchange rates simply level the playing field. . . . Clearly, neither Visa nor MasterCard is content to allow the other the high ground, particularly as large issuers are deciding if they even want to stay with either association."

16. See letter from Bruce Mansfield, General Manager, Visa International, Australia & New Zealand, to John Veale, Head of Payments Policy, Reserve Bank of

Australia, April 7, 2005 (www.rba.gov.au/PaymentsSystem/Reforms/CCSchemes/ SubmissionsCCIStd/visa_07042005_1.pdf).

17. Ibid.

18. See also Alan S. Frankel and Allan L. Shampine, "The Economic Effects of Interchange Fees," *Antitrust Law Journal* 73, no. 3: 627–73.

19. This proposal might be implementable by enforcement of existing antitrust laws against unreasonable restraint of trade. However, to avoid the delays and uncertainties of adjudication it may be simpler to enact legislation to ensure that contracts between card networks, merchants, acquiring banks, and issuing banks do not restrict the ability of merchants to preferentially steer (through pricing or otherwise) customers to a particular card network (Visa versus MasterCard versus AMEX); to a particular product of the card network (for example, debit rather than credit card); or to a particular issuer bank of the same card network (say, Citibank Visa versus Chase Visa).

20. See Frankel and Shampine, p. 641.

21. See Howard Chang, David Evans, and Daniel D. Garcia-Swartz, "The Effect of Regulatory Intervention in Two-Sided Markets: An Assessment of Interchange-Fee Capping in Australia," *Review of Network Economics* 4, no. 4 (2005): 329.

22. See Alan S. Frankel, "Toward a Competitive Card Payments Marketplace," mimeo, 2006, p. 32.

23. See Reserve Bank of Australia, Payments System Board, 2005 Annual Report, pp. 10–11.

24. Chang, Evans, and Garcia-Swartz reported a 60 to 70 percent reduction in the overall cost of transactions in the economy since card issuers have recovered 30 to 40 percent of the lost interchange fee revenue by charging higher fees to cardholders. See also Frankel, p. 37.

THOMAS P. BROWN

7

Keeping Electronic Money Valuable: The Future of Payments and the Role of Public Authorities

The weekend of September 13–14, 2008, we watched a long-simmering financial crisis boil over. One institution that seemed to define financial stability disappeared; another sold itself for approximately 60 percent of the price it would have commanded a year ago;[1] and a third was hastily rescued by the federal government.[2] Coming out of these events, it is tempting to say that the next wave to break will come in the payments industry, and that the federal government must immediately do something to stop the impending crisis. After all, more attention in Congress means more work for lawyers and law professors.

But it would be wrong to give in to this temptation. There is no looming crisis in the payments industry. The payments industry has held up remarkably well amidst the biggest financial crisis since the Great Depression. The current problems originate in the consumer credit industry, and firms in the credit business as well as the payment business, such as American Express, have suffered.[3] But firms that manage just the exchange of value have, so far, avoided the worst of it.[4]

This recent experience suggests a different path—arguing that the government stay out of this industry altogether. Some, of course, find

I would like to thank Will Trachman of O'Melveny & Myers for his excellent research assistance.

127

the notion of regulation and supervision of any industry abhorrent. To be sure, regulation can do more harm than good. The risk looms particularly large in an industry as dynamic and innovative as modern consumer payments. But even classical liberals recognize a role for the government in preventing force and fraud from affecting the interaction between otherwise private actors.[5] Once the threshold of permitting some role for the government is crossed, the challenge becomes marking the proper boundary between helpful and unhelpful regulation.

Drawing this line is challenging in any industry, but it is especially challenging in payments. Tim Muris has described the payment card as one of the great innovations of the twentieth century—on a par with the microchip, cell phone, and personal computer.[6] Like them, the payment card has transformed modern life to the point where modern consumer payments are taken almost completely for granted. A business trip triggers a series of transactions that most consumers barely notice: buying airline tickets, reserving a hotel room, renting a car, and so on. These transactions are mundane, however, only because payment cards have made these otherwise complicated transactions safe, reliable, and, from the consumer's perspective, free. It was not always so. Furthermore, any workable framework for regulating and supervising this industry must be grounded in a solid understanding of how it has evolved.

The Early History of Payments

In human terms, payments are a comparatively new development. Most Western historians date the emergence of a true payment system to the seventh century BCE and, like Herodotus, credit the Lydians with creating the first—the coin.[7] Unlike some of the other technologies that shape modern life, such as advances in transportation, communications, and information processing, it is not immediately obvious how society benefits from advancements in the means of value exchange. Payments are, after all, an adjunct to trade, and trade was a feature of human society long before the Lydians struck the first coin. But the dynamics that prompted the move from barter to more sophisticated means of value exchange continue to shape the industry.

It seems obvious that the very first humans engaged in some form of direct trading with one another—probably a deal like *my eggs for your animal skins*. Unfortunately, direct exchange has severe limitations as a means of exchanging value. First, if the other party to the exchange already has the thing that the first party wants to trade, the two sides may be unable to strike a deal—*if you already have eggs, you won't give me animal skins*. Second, the value of some items is difficult to preserve over time—*eventually eggs go bad*. Third, the cost of maintaining a network of direct connections increases rapidly as the number of people in the network grows; or, put slightly differently, direct exchange does not scale. Only three links are needed to connect three people (think of the vertices of a triangle); but when the number of people in the network grows to ten, the number of links needed to connect all the participants grows to forty-five.[8] The efficiencies captured by a switch from a system of direct exchange to an agreed-upon medium are equivalent to those captured by routing telephone calls through an exchange rather than by laying a separate wire for each pair of individuals who might want to be connected.[9]

This last point simply restates one of the basic principles of network economics, but its importance to understanding the payments industry cannot be overstated.[10] It helps explain the evolution of payment from the concrete media of exchange that prevailed in the ancient world (domesticated animals, precious metals, and slaves) to the abstract forms of payment that are now ubiquitous (paper money, checks, and electrons). But this principle has a double edge. When the value of a system is tied to its size, attracting and keeping a critical mass of users is a life-or-death proposition. Defections from a particular form of payment by some users can lead others to look for alternatives.[11]

Modern Consumer Payments

Today, payments are big business. Global industry transactions across all forms of payment products and services for consumers and business exceeded $1.7 trillion in 2007.[12] The industry is now larger than the lodging, airline, computer software, personal computer, and movie industries. And it has grown to this size in a remarkably short time.

The modern payments industry got its start in 1948 when Frank McNamara introduced the first true general-purpose payment card system, Diners Club.[13] The industry grew quickly as the likes of American Express, Bank of America, Citibank, and others saw the potential in McNamara's concept. Network economics shaped the rivalries among these firms. Over the past sixty years, they have worked to attract new users and increase the value of the system to existing users. And competition has played out across three key dimensions: products, points of sale, and processing.

Products

This year marks the fiftieth anniversary of what we know now as Visa.[14] The company began as an extension of the consumer lending business built by A. P. Giannini, the founder of Bank of America. Giannini believed that immigrant farmers and fisherman could be trusted to manage their income and their expenses, and gave them the opportunity to take out small loans to buy tools, clothes, and other consumer goods according to their needs rather than when the crab season opened or walnuts ripened on trees. This democratization of consumer credit led directly to the mainstream introduction of credit cards.[15]

Bank of America launched its BancAmericard system to give consumers and—just as important—small merchants the ability to tap into a line of credit extended by a bank without having to repeatedly go back to a loan officer to approve each new purchase. With general-purpose cards, consumers enjoyed more financial freedom. So did merchants, who could leave the business of extending credit and making collections to others so that they could focus on selling merchandise.

Visa's first major corporate reorganization—its spin-off from Bank of America—extended the vision of these two programs. Dee Hock, the CEO of Visa, believed that the terms on which consumers settled up with the issuing bank should be irrelevant to everyone but the consumer and the issuer, and he pushed the company to launch what was the first general-purpose debit card program in the United States.[16] Since then, the initial vision of a credit card has expanded into four major product categories: credit, debit, commercial, and prepaid.

Prepaid is the most recent addition. Its rapid growth (it is the fastest growing product category in the Visa lineup) illustrates how modern payment systems are constantly striving to expand their reach. Prepaid cards embrace a wide range of products that share one characteristic—funds are deposited before payment is made. This substantially reduces credit risk, making it possible to extend the reach of the card networks to people outside the financial mainstream. Prepaid cards have enabled networks to penetrate payment categories that have traditionally relied on paper, including rebates, health care, travel, and, of course, gift certificates.[17]

Prepaid cards also have the potential to revolutionize how governments distribute benefits. Many states and federal agencies have used prepaid cards to replace checks to disburse funds such as child support, unemployment insurance, workers' compensation benefits, and other benefits programs.[18] This switch has saved millions of dollars in administrative costs. In Colorado, for instance, the state saved nearly $210,000 in postage alone by switching its unemployment insurance payments from paper checks to prepaid cards.[19]

Points of Sale

Payment systems have dramatically expanded the universe of places where cards may be used. When Diners Club launched the first payment card system in 1950, its cards could be used in only a handful of restaurant locations in New York. And when Bank of America launched the predecessor to the Visa system, the acceptance network was limited geographically—to Fresno—and to a fairly limited group of merchants—boutique retailers who could not afford to offer credit to their customers.

Since then, though, the various systems have spent millions overcoming these limitations and expanding their networks. The expansions tended to occur in waves: department stores in the 1970s, supermarkets and drugstores in the 1980s and 1990s. The most recent expansion has focused on quick service restaurants (QSR).[20] Persuading new groups of merchants to accept cards meant that payment card companies needed to figure out the appropriate balance of economics for a particular and unique retail environment. Merchants such as In-and-Out had historically objected to accepting cards, in large part because collecting signatures on every transaction lengthened the lines at the counter and slowed service. In response, networks changed their rules for small-ticket purchases—by waiving the requirement to collect signatures—and QSR acceptance has since flourished. Even McDonald's, one of the most sophisticated merchants in the world, has lauded the value of card acceptance in terms of faster turnaround at the register and higher revenue.[21]

Processing

Processing is the final important dimension of competition. This, however, tends to be the least obvious to consumers. From the consumer perspective (at least in the United States), payment cards work today as they have for decades. Give the card to the merchant, wait for the machine to beep, sign the slip, and leave. But changes in how transactions are processed can be just as important as expanding the network or increasing the variety of card types. And the emergence of PayPal shows how seemingly small changes in processing can open up new opportunities for expansion.

Historically, when consumers used payment cards, they had to give the card, with the data either embossed on the card or encrypted on the magnetic stripe, to the merchant. This proved a major obstacle to the use of such cards as the Internet took off. This was particularly true in environments such as eBay, where consumers were completing transactions with people they neither knew nor saw. Consumers were understandably reluctant to trust strangers with data that could be used to generate fraudulent transactions.

PayPal developed an innovative way to solve this problem. It signed up merchants and consumers, and developed a protocol to complete the exchange of value by instruction rather than the direct exchange of information. A consumer using PayPal exchanges value with a merchant that accepts PayPal by instructing PayPal to move that value from his or her PayPal account into the merchant's account. In the PayPal system, the consumer's account information does not have to change hands. By establishing itself as a reliable and trustworthy intermediary for payments, PayPal eliminated the need for individual strangers to trust each other in that context. Instead, they could reasonably trust that PayPal would transfer funds only in accordance with users' desires, and would do so in a way that kept private data private.

An Appropriate Role for Authorities

The connection between this short history of payments and the role that public authorities should take with regard to the payments industry may not be obvious. But two general points extracted from this crash course in the history of payments provide a framework for analyzing the role that the government can usefully play in this industry.

First, people will use a payment system only if they trust that other people are going to use it. Modern consumer payment systems have lost any vestige of the intrinsic value (such as eggs, animal skins, gold, or other precious metals) long thought to be essential to the success of a payment system. The electrons that are charged to your credit card are the physical manifestation of a typical point-of-sale transaction that, like the $20 bill, has no intrinsic utility. Payment card systems and paper money work as means to exchange value only because each user has confidence that they are going to work.

The second point is simply a corollary of the first: competition drives innovation in this industry. Consumers may not notice each incremental innovation, but they notice the accumulation of incremental investments. They also consistently use the systems that they find to be safe, efficient, and reliable. Payment systems that do not improve lose out, over time, to those that do. Whatever role the government plays, it must avoid suppressing the incentive to innovate.

This response assumes that the government is in fact going to play a role in this industry. And that is a safe assumption. The U.S. Constitution puts the federal government squarely in the business of the payments industry with the power to coin and regulate money. And the federal government, through the Federal Reserve, is an established and major player in the business. It manages the two consumer payment systems—cash and check—that together clear more value than all other systems combined.

The role that the federal government plays in supervising the cash and check systems clearly instills public confidence in the integrity and reliability of those systems. There is every reason to believe that the federal government could play a similar role for other systems. As the Treasury Department's *Blueprint for a Modernized Financial Regulatory Structure* recognizes, the federal government is truly unique in this regard.[22] The mere fact of government oversight can help financial institutions build and maintain public confidence, particularly in times of financial stress. Supervision does not mean micromanagement, however, and it is, unfortunately, easy to miss the thin line that separates one from the other.

The various responses to the high-profile theft of payment card data and other information from large merchants illustrate the limits on useful government intervention in the industry. Electronic payment card systems have become quite secure. Fraud rates on the Visa system have dropped more than 20 percent in the past ten years. The payment card industry—American Express, Discover, MasterCard, and Visa—has also developed a standard to make the systems even more secure. Nevertheless, systems do remain vulnerable to certain types of attacks. In particular, if thieves capture the full contents of the magnetic stripe on the back of a card, they can use the information to create counterfeit cards that elude detection.

The government's productive role in addressing this problem was revealed on August 5, 2008. That day, the U.S. attorneys of Massachusetts, the Eastern District of New York, and the Southern District of California accused eleven people of hacking into the systems of nine retailers, most prominently TJX, over a five-year period. The investigation (as well as the crime) was truly breathtaking:

—The defendants hacked into the retailer computer systems and inserted "sniffers" to intercept card numbers, as well as PINs, used to initiate PIN debit card transactions.

—They cashed out by selling the numbers to criminals around the globe and using the intercepted PINs to withdraw tens of thousands of dollars at a time from ATMs.

—One of the defendants, Maksym Yastremskiy, allegedly pocketed $11 million dollars as a result of the coordinated criminal activity.

—The defendants were from five countries: the United States, Estonia, Ukraine, China, and Belarus.

—Several arrests took place in the United States, Germany, and Turkey.

Only the federal government could have investigated and prosecuted a case of this size and sophistication. As U.S. Attorney General Michael Mukasey explained when the indictments were revealed, "This is the single largest and most complex identity theft case ever charged in this country." The investigation, he continued, also "shows that, with the cooperation of our law enforcement partners around the world, we can identify, charge and apprehend even the most sophisticated international computer hackers."[23]

Unfortunately, however, governments, both state and federal, have not confined their interest in security breaches to prosecuting the people who commit them. All the major systems have rules for distributing the costs of fraud between the merchants that accept cards and the financial institutions that issue those cards.[24] For various reasons, smaller financial institutions have suffered unreimbursed fraud losses disproportionate to their share of total volume. They have also attempted to bypass the networks' dispute resolution regimes with lawsuits. For the most part, though, courts have rightly rejected those claims, and smaller financial institutions have instead begun to lobby state legislatures to adopt laws shifting liability for such losses entirely to merchants. Some state legislatures, including Minnesota, have obliged.[25]

The financial institutions that have pushed for these laws to be adopted have a point. Many merchants could do more to prevent theft of live cardholder data, and those steps would cut down on fraud losses.

But strict liability rules of the sort adopted in Minnesota and elsewhere simply are not the answer. The responsibility to prevent fraud does not end when someone steals card data. Financial institutions can take steps to prevent thieves from converting data into dollars, and state legislatures should not relieve them of that responsibility. Private payment networks have every incentive to strike the right balance. Government at all levels should allow them to do so.[26]

This discussion leads inevitably to the other big topic looming on the public agenda for the payment business—who should bear the cost of payments. There is not space enough here to explore this topic in full, but as people make up their minds on the question, it is worth noting that the United States has twice tried to regulate the costs. Both times the intervention failed.

During the Civil War, the federal government tried to force state banks to adopt the newly created federal charter by imposing punitive taxes on their bank notes. State banks stopped issuing notes, but managed to stay in business without taking a federal charter. They devised a novel product that enabled consumers to pay bills without buying notes—the checking account. The checking account, in its first iteration, featured the same discount when deposited by the recipient that had largely fueled the objection to bank notes.[27]

In the early part of the twentieth century, the federal government again tried to force the market to re-price payment services. This time the target was discount fees on checks, and the campaign can be traced directly to William Jennings Bryan's famous Cross of Gold speech.[28] Essentially, Bryan wanted the federal government to simply set the price of payments.[29] About ten years later, following the 1907 bank panic, the federal government tried to do exactly that by creating the Federal Reserve and using it to attempt to implement par exchange of checks. The Fed eventually succeeded, but not until 1970.[30] By the time it did, another payment instrument had emerged that required the acceptor to pay a discount on the face value of the transaction—the general purpose payment card.

Conclusion

The consensus, on all sides, is that the payment industry is dynamic, and will continue to evolve to meet the demands of financial institutions, consumers, and merchants. Systems—like Visa's—are a critical piece of the nation's dynamic and evolving economic infrastructure. Society gains when inefficient legacy payment systems such as cash and check give way to electronic payments. Earlier this year, the Department of Commerce observed that "electronic payments have the potential to provide cost savings of at least 1 percent of GDP annually over paper-based systems through increased velocity, reduced friction, and lower costs."[31]

That government recognizes the value of the electronic payment systems is critical to the future. Government authorities obviously have an interest in supervising payment systems. In addition, there is indeed a role for government agencies in maintaining a well-functioning and modern payment system, and an important role at that. No commercial entity is in the same kind of position to help protect the integrity of—and maintain trust in—payments like public authorities.

But the government's role, though a necessary one, should be focused on protecting the integrity of these systems by, for example, punishing people who commit fraud. It must resist the temptation to manage private payment systems. Payment systems connect thousands of financial institutions, millions of merchants, and tens of millions of consumers that define modern payments. No regulatory system, however well-intentioned, can efficiently manage systems that are this complex and dynamic.

Notes

1. The three events are, of course, the collapse of Lehman, the sale of Merrill Lynch, and the bailout of AIG. See, generally, Christine Harper, "'Tectonic' Market Shift as Lehman Fails, Merrill Sold," Bloomberg.com, September 15, 2008 (www.bloomberg.com/apps/news?pid=20601087&sid=abVpg8xJDMWk&refer=home); see also Merrill Lynch Stockchart (www.wikinvest.com/stock/Merrill_Lynch _(MER)/WikiChart).

2. See Ben Feller, "White House Defends Takeover of AIG," *Manchester Guardian*, September 17, 2008.

3. See Robin Sidel, "Delinquencies Mount for American Express," October 20, 2008 (http://online.wsj.com/article/SB122446082980748593.html?mod=google news_wsj).

4. See Adam Frisch, "Battleships Do Better in Choppy Seas," UBS Investment Research, October 30, 2008.

5. Richard A. Epstein and Thomas P. Brown, "The War on Plastic," *Regulation* 29, no. 3 (Fall 2006): 12–16.

6. See, for example, Timothy J. Muris, "Payment Card Regulation and The (Mis)Application of the Economics of Two-Sided Markets," *Columbia Business Law Review* 515 (2005) (Exhibit B); Timothy J. Muris, "What's in Your Wallet?" *Wall Street Journal*, June 24, 2005, p. A12.

7. David S. Evans and Richard Schmalensee, *Paying with Plastic: The Digital Revolution in Buying and Borrowing* (MIT Press, 2005), 27.

8. In any network, the number of pairs of connections is equal to $(N*(N-1)/2)$. See Robert A. Hanneman and Mark Riddle, "Introduction to Social Networks" (University of California–Riverside, 2005) (www.faculty.ucr.edu/~hanneman/nettext).

9. Epstein and Brown, "The War on Plastic," 13.

10. Evans and Schmalensee, *Paying with Plastic*, 35–36.

11. David S. Evans, "The Antitrust Economics of Multi-Sided Platform Markets," *Yale Journal of Regulation* 20, no. 2 (2003): 325–81; see also Evans and Schmalensee, *Paying with Plastic*, 53–56.

12. Evans and Schmalensee, *Paying with Plastic*, 1–3.

13. Ibid., 53–56.

14. Ibid., 14. Additionally, as noted by Ken Chenault in chapter 5, this is also the fiftieth anniversary of American Express.

15. Lendol Calder, *Financing the American Dream: A Cultural History of Consumer Credit* (Princeton University Press, 1999); Tom Brown and Lacey Plache, "Paying with Plastic: Maybe Not So Crazy," *University of Chicago Law Review* 73 (Winter 2006): 63–86.

16. Evans and Schmalensee, *Paying with Plastic*, 206–10.

17. "ThankYou Network Introduces Greater Flexibility with the Inclusion of Prepaid Cards in Its Reward Collection," *Market Watch (WSJ)*, October 15, 2008, www.marketwatch.com/news/story/thankyour-network-introduces-greater-flexibility/story.aspx?guid=%7B1EB2DE73-BEF2-4EBC-94DF-A5F67F C83393%7D&dist=hppr.

18. Direct Payment Card (DPC) Application, Alaska Child Support Services Division, Department of Revenue, www.csed.state.ak.us/Debit%20Card/04-0006 %20Debit_card_authorization.pdf.

19. See John Morell, "Unemployment Benefits Switch from Paper to Plastic," Creditcards.com, July 21, 2008, www.creditcards.com/credit-card-news/unemployment-benefits-debit-cards-1271.php.

20. Gregory Holmes, "QSR Operators Play Their Cards Right by Allowing Electronic Credit, Debit Payments," *Nation's Restaurant News*, October 17, 2005 (www.findarticles.com/p/articles/mi_m3190/is_42_39/ai_n15727987).

21. See Anupama Chandrasekaran, "McDonald's Embraces Plastic for Its Restaurants," Reuters, March 26, 2004 (www.usatoday.com/money/industries/food/2004-03-26-mcdonalds-credit_x.htm).

22. See U.S. Department of the Treasury, Press Room Reports, March 31, 2008 (www.treasury.gov/press/releases/reports/Blueprint.pdf).

23. Department of Justice, "Retail Hacking Ring Charged for Stealing and Distributing Credit and Debit Card Numbers from Major U.S. Retailers," press release, August 5, 2008 (www.usdoj.gov/opa/pr/2008/August/08-ag-689.html).

24. See Richard A. Epstein and Thomas P. Brown, "Cybersecurity in the Payment Card Industry," *University of Chicago Law Review* 75 (Winter 2008): 203–24.

25. Ibid.

26. Ibid.

27. Oliver Ireland and Rachel Howell, "The Evolving Payments Landscape," *Journal of Payment Systems Law* 1 (2005): 524, 525.

28. For the text of the speech, see History Matters (http://historymatters.gmu.edu/d/5354). For an audio recording, see Joe Richman, "William Jennings Bryan: An Electrifying Orator," National Public Radio, October 14, 2008 (www.npr.org/templates/story/story.php?storyId=95691800).

29. Richman, "William Jennings Bryan." "I stand with Jefferson rather than with them, and tell them, as he did, that the issue of money is a function of the government and that the banks should go out of the governing business."

30. Evans and Schmalensee, *Paying with Plastic*, 39–42.

31. Scott Schmith, "Credit Card Market: Economic Benefits and Industry Trends," Office Publication (U.S. Department of Commerce, International Trade Administration, March 2008), p. 2 (www.ita.doc.gov/td/finance/publications/credit cards.pdf).

Contributors

MARTIN NEIL BAILY
Brookings Institution

THOMAS P. BROWN
O'Melveny & Myers

KENNETH CHENAULT
American Express Company

VIJAY D'SILVA
McKinsey and Company

NICHOLAS ECONOMIDES
New York University

DAVID S. EVANS
Market Platform Dynamics

ROBERT E. LITAN
*Kauffman Foundation and
    Brookings Institution*

DRAZEN PRELEC
*Massachusetts Institute of
    Technology*

RICHARD SCHMALENSEE
*Massachusetts Institute of
    Technology*

Index

ACHs. *See* Automated clearinghouses

ATMs. *See* Automated teller machines

Advertising industry, 12, 54–57, 69, 70, 71

Africa, 64. *See also* Kenya

American Express, 6–7, 102–03, 106, 109–10, 113, 114, 127. *See also* Credit cards—specific

Antitrust suit, 16, 72, 76n55, 118, 120, 124n7

API. *See* Application programming interface

Apple, 61–62, 70

Application programming interface (API), 67

Australia, 123

Austria, 63

Automated clearinghouses (ACHs): electronic payments and, 66; processing ACH transactions, 28–29; use of checks and cash and, 10, 26

Automated teller machines (ATMs), 8, 21

Bank of America, 6–7, 28–29, 130. *See also* Credit cards—specific; Visa

Banks and banking: acquiring banks, 16, 114–15, 116, 120, 121, 122; checks and, 5, 10, 20, 26, 41, 136; consolidation of the banking industry, 10; consumer data and, 69; currency and, 20; costs of, 9, 26; credit cards and, 16; debit cards and, 8; digital check imaging and, 26; history and background of, 4–5; Internet banking, 8; issuing banks, 16, 114–15, 121, 122; MasterCard and Visa and, 113; on-us transactions, 28; remote deposit capture and, 26–27; strategies for, 34–35; subsidies to, 72. *See also individual banks*

Beenz, 32

Bellamy, Edward, 20

BillMeLater, 12, 15, 52, 106

Blueprint for a Modernized Financial Regulatory Structure (Treasury Department), 134

Brazil, 108

BRIC countries. *See* Brazil; Russia; India; China

Brown, Thomas P., 16–17, 127–39

Bryan, William Jennings, 136

Business issues: business models, 34, 53, 66; fraud and trust, 33, 104, 109–12, 133; investment process and risk, 33; organization, 33; value creation, 68

Cardlytics, 59

Carte Blanche payment card, 6

Cellfire, 59

Celtel (Africa), 64

Chase Paymentech, 38

Checkclearing for the 21st Century Act (Check 21; 2004), 26, 27f

Checks. *See* Banks and banking

Check 21. *See* Checkclearing for the 21st Century Act

Chenault, Kenneth, 15, 102–12

China, 108, 109

Civil War, 136

Clearinghouses, 5. *See also* Automated clearing houses

Club Med, 14, 83

CNN.com, 54

Colorado, 131

Commerce, Department of, 137

Competition. *See* Economic issues

Constitution (U.S.), 16

Consumers: ambivalence toward credit cards, 88; attitudes toward costs and payment, 77, 78–79; cashless society and, 107–08; consumer demand for new technologies, 105; consumer protection, 70–71; consumer surplus, 68; contactless payment systems and, 51–52; costs and, 118; decisionmaking by, 87, 94; development of payments systems and, 78; fees and, 116, 117; future of consumer payments, 102–12; inertia of, 31, 33, 35, 39–40, 48–53; mashups and, 68–72; online advertising and, 54; Pay By Touch and, 50; prepayment and, 81–82; rational consumers, 80; transaction data of, 53–60, 70, 71; view of payment experiences, 39–40, 94; wireless/mobile phone technologies and, 12, 64–65. *See also* Psychological issues

Consumption, 13–15, 79–86

CPC (cost-per-click), 54

Credit cards: addictive consumption by, 90–91; attitudes toward, 88, 89–90; background and history of, 6–8, 16, 20–21, 37–38, 130; benefits of, 78; business model of, 6–7; contactless payments, 10–11, 12, 29, 31, 36, 40, 42, 44t, 50–51; costs of, 9, 15, 32, 46–47; debit cards and, 78, 97n2; delay of payments for, 88; economic value of consumer data, 57–60; federal liability limit, 9; fees and pricing of, 15, 16, 33, 34, 41, 53, 113, 114, 115, 118; fraud and deceptive practices and, 33, 70, 134–36; market shares of, 124n4; moral tax of, 14; multiparty card associations, 114; origin of payment card networks, 37–39; outstanding debt of, 7; popularity of, 13, 40; processors of, 38; products of, 130–31; signing of, 52; smart cards, 28, 32; subsidization of, 120; transaction data from, 70; transaction-related services and, 65; transaction time of, 39; trust and, 33; universal default of, 15, 110. *See also*

Payments; Payments systems;
Rules
Credit cards—specific: American
Express, 6–7, 15, 16, 20, 47, 59,
72, 113, 114, 134; BankAmericard, 20, 130, 131; Diners Club,
6, 20, 47, 131; Discover Card
(Sears), 6, 7, 28, 47, 113, 134; Edy
(Japan), 32; MasterCard, 7, 16,
28, 38, 41, 47, 51, 52, 69, 72,
113, 114, 117, 122, 134; Octopus
card (Hong Kong), 31, 50–51;
Oyster card (U.K.), 28, 31; RevolutionCard (U.S.), 32; Speedpass
(ExxonMobile), 28; Squid (U.K.),
32; Visa card (Bank of America),
7, 16, 20, 28, 38, 41, 47, 51, 69,
72, 113, 114, 117, 122, 134. *See
also individual card companies*
Customers. *See* Consumers
CVS, 51

Debit cards. *See* Payments systems
Diners Club card, 6, 20
Discover, 106. *See also* Credit
cards—specific
D'Silva, Vijay, 10–11, 19–35

eBay, 32, 132
Economic issues: adoption of new
payment methods, 45–49; barter,
3, 128–29; coin and paper money,
3–4, 128–29; competition, 69,
102, 106, 108, 109, 113–24, 130,
133; consumer surplus, 68; developing economies, 108; economic
efficiency, 93–97; exchange of
value, 132–33; generation of
value, 68; global commerce,
111–12; growth, 107; human
capital investment, 48; improving
efficiency, 121–22; incremental

sales, 51, 52; market power, 116;
medium of exchange, 1; monetiz-
ing transaction data, 57–60; monopoly, 122; network economics,
129; store of value, 1; sunk
investments, 48; trade, 129; trust,
109, 133; tying, 120; unit of
account, 1. *See also* Money
Economides, Nicholas, 15–16,
113–26
Edy (Japan). *See* Credit cards—
specific
Efficiency, 121–22
EFT (Electronic Funds Transfer Act;
1978), 32
Electronic payment cards. *See* Credit
cards; Payments systems
Equipment: cash-dispensing
machines, 41; point-of-sale devices, 38, 39, 41, 49, 51; subsidization of, 41
Europe, 5, 6, 8, 31, 63
Evans, David, 9, 11–13, 36–76
E-ZPass, 10–11, 31

Facebook, 54, 57
Fargo, William, 103. *See also* Wells
Fargo
Federal Reserve System (Fed): check
clearing and, 20; credit card
practices and, 104, 110–12;
financial crises and, 5; history and
background of, 4–5, 136; role of,
17, 134
Fees: card network fees, 123; consumer fees, 116, 117; interchange
fees, 16, 41, 72, 76n55, 115–16,
120, 122, 123; transaction facilitation fees, 117–20; transaction
fees, 114, 115–16. *See also* Credit
cards; Merchants
Financial crises, 5, 10, 136

Fingerprints, 49–50
First Data Corporation, 38
Frequency programs, 14, 83–84, 96

GCASH (Philippines), 64
Giannini, A. P., 130
Giro payments systems, 5–6, 8
Global positioning system (GPS), 29–30, 62–63
Google, Gmail, and Google Checkout, 30, 56, 57, 59, 62, 70
Governments: innovation and, 133; preservation of public confidence and, 17, 110; role in the payments industry, 16–17, 134, 136, 137; use of prepaid cards, 16, 131. *See also* Public policy
GPS. *See* Global positioning system
Great Depression, 5

Hedonic buffers, 83
Hilton Hotels, 6
Hock, Dee, 130
Hong Kong, 31, 50–51

Ikobo, 31
In-and-Out, 132
India, 23, 64, 108, 109
Indochina, 109
Inertia. *See* Consumers
Internet: banking, 8; "cloud-based computing," 40–41, 65–68; cookies on the, 56, 58; mobile phones and, 60–61; online advertising industry, 54–57; online spending, 108; payments systems and, 9, 107–08; protocol development and, 41. *See also* BillMeLater
IP Commerce, 66–67
iPhone, 61–62
iPod, 62

Japan: credit cards in, 32; payments systems in, 23; wireless/mobile payments systems in, 8, 10, 30, 33, 63, 64

Kenya, 63. *See also* Africa
Kivetz, Ran, 84
Korea, 63

Lawsuit, antitrust, 16, 72, 76n55, 118, 120
Leasing, 95
Legal issues, 71
Linux, 62
London (U.K.), 31
Looking Backward (Bellamy), 20

Mac OS X, 62
Mashups. *See* Payments industry; Technological issues
MasterCard, 38, 52, 113, 119. *See also* Credit cards–specific
McDonald's, 51, 132
mChek (India), 64
McNamara, Frank, 130
Merchants: adoption of new methods, 12, 40, 42, 45–53; BillMeLater and, 52; card contracts and, 121; contactless systems and, 51, 64; costs and, 32, 45–47, 118; consumer data and, 69; credit card rules and, 15–16, 118; fees and, 16, 40, 46–47, 113, 115–16, 118, 119, 120, 121, 122, 123–24; inertia and, 48–53; liability for fraud and, 135–36; mashups and, 68–72; mobile phones and, 64; networks and, 38; payments systems and, 23, 32, 113, 114; remote deposit capture and, 26–27; systems revenues and, 72

McKinsey and Company, 10
Minnesota, 135, 136
Money, 1, 3–9, 113
Moral tax, 14, 79–86, 93, 94–96, 98n4
Morgan, J. P., 4
M-Pesa technology. *See* Technologies
Mukasey, Michael, 135
Muris, Tim, 128

Near Field Communication (NFC), 30, 36
Netflix, 14, 86–87
Networks: connection of client computers and, 40; consolidation of, 28–29; costs of, 117, 123, 129; closed networks, 27, 28; economics of, 129; expansion of, 131–32; fees and, 113, 117–20, 122, 123; growth and development of, 29, 38–39, 48; interoperability of computer networks, 41; open networks, 27–28; payment/credit card networks, 37–39, 40, 65–66, 117; prepaid cards and, 131; private networks, 38; software for, 38–39; strategies of, 117–18; three- and four-party networks, 114–17
Neuroscience of shopping, 91–92
NFC. *See* Near Field Communications
NTT DOCOMO (Japan), 30, 32

Olympic Games (*1996*; Atlanta, GA), 32

Palm OS, 62
Pariter Solutions, 28–29
Path dependence, 48–49, 60
Paybox (Austria), 63
Pay By Touch, 32, 49–50, 53

Payforit (U.K.), 63
Payments: background and history of, 128–29; banking revenues and, 21; cash and, 41; consumer attitudes toward, 77, 78–79; costs of, 86–88, 136; elimination of uncovered payments, 86–87; form factor/physical method of, 36–37, 53, 64; future of consumer payments, 102–12; modern consumer payments, 129–33; person-to-person payments, 31–32; pleasure of consumption and, 13–15; prepayment, 14; processing of, 21–23, 38, 132–33; uncovered payments, 87. *See also* Moral tax
Payments industry: background and development of, 19–21, 128–30; creative destruction of, 72n1; definitions of, 105f; electronic payments industry, 73n4; future of, 10–17, 102–12; issues of, 1–2; lack of crisis in, 127; mashups of payments, technologies, and business models, 12, 36–37, 40; megatrends in, 23–32; mobile phones and, 64–65; payments instruments and pathways, 10, 21–23, 104–05; regulation of, 127–28; software platforms and, 66–68; strategies for, 34–35; as a two-sided platform, 45; value chain of, 21–23. *See also* Banks and banking; Money
Payments systems: bundling/financial coupling, 84–85, 99n24; business models for, 82; cash and currency in, 20, 24f, 41, 43, 44–45, 107, 120; characteristics of, 8–9, 104–05; checks and checking, 5, 23–24, 32, 41, 107; "in the cloud

computing" and, 41; contactless payments, 10–11, 12, 29, 31, 36, 40, 42, 44t, 50–51, 64, 74n29; costs and fees of, 9, 26, 34, 52; debit cards, 8–13, 14–15, 16, 20–21, 78, 97n2, 119, 130–31, 135; design of, 93; digital checks and money, 26, 42; direct transfer systems, 5–6, 24; electronic payments, 10, 15, 20–21, 42, 66, 73n4, 107–09, 113, 137; fixed payment plans/subscriptions, 85–86; giro payment systems, 5, 8; innovation and improvement in, 133; installment payments, 81–82; Internet/online payment mechanisms, 8, 9, 10, 21, 24, 52; magnetic stripe cards, 37, 40, 41, 42, 43–44, 51, 134; mobile and wireless payments systems, 8, 12–13, 63–65; new instruments and entrants in, 29–32, 43–44; open and closed networks, 10, 27–29; paper-based transactions, 23–24, 26; payment cards, 45, 65–66; payment rails, 66, 676; payments networks (open and closed), 27–29; person-to-person payments, 31–32; points of sale, 131–32; prepayment and prepaid cards, 13, 16, 32, 78, 81–83, 97n3, 98n11, 131; prix fixe payments, 83; processing, 132–33; remote deposit capture, 26; security of, 9, 64; token currencies, 83. *See also* Credit cards

PayPal, 8, 11, 15, 32, 66, 106, 132–33
PaySimple, 67
Philippines, 32, 64
Prelec, Drazen, 13, 77–101

Prepayment. *See* Payments; Payments systems
Price regulation, 71–72
Privacy issues, 56–57, 71
Processing. *See* Payments
Processors. *See* Credit cards
Psychological issues: "chicken-and-egg" problem, 12; coupling, 84–85, 99n24; delay-of-gratification, 100n28; double-entry mental accounting, 82, 86–88; fixed versus variable payment plans, 85–86; hedonic or economic efficiency, 93–97; inertia, 9, 11, 48–53; methods of payment and, 2, 90; moral tax and payments, 79–86; paternalism, 96–97; self-control, 89–97, 92–93, 97n3; transaction coupling, 88; trust, 15, 109. *See also* Consumers
Public policies: change and, 37; competition issues in the payments industry, 113–24; online advertising and, 56; payments and, 11; policymakers and mashups, 68–72; promotion of payments innovation and, 13; regulation of payments costs, 136. *See also* Governments

Quick service restaurants (QSRs), 132

RBA. *See* Reserve Bank of Australia
Research InMotion, 62
Reserve Bank of Australia (RBA), 123
Revolution Money, 53, 75n33
Rules, 123–24
Rules—specific: distribution of costs of fraud, 135–36; honor all cards,

16, 117, 118, 119–20; maximum interchange fees, 16; most-favored-customer, 118; no-discrimination, 119, 121, 123–24; no-surcharge, 118–19, 121, 123–24, 125n12; steering, 15, 16, 123
Russia, 108

Safaricom, 63
Sales. *See* Economic issues
Schmalensee, Richard, 9, 11–13, 36–76
Search engines. *See* Technologies
Sears, 6, 7, 47. *See also* Credit Cards—specific
7-Eleven, 51
Short Message Service (SMS), 30–31, 63–64
Simonson, Itamar, 84
SMS. *See* Short Message Service
Squid (U.K.), 32
Symbian, 62

Targeting, 55–59, 69
Technological issues: barriers to innovation and success, 33–34, 39–40, 44–45, 52–53; consumer demand and, 105; cost and convenience of payments cards, 11–12; development of the payments cards, 16; digital imaging, 10; emerging payment instruments and entrants, 29–32, 63–65, 107; technology failures, 32; innovation, 39, 43–53; mashups of payments, technologies, and business models, 12, 36–37, 40, 42, 53, 59, 60, 64–65, 67–72, 73n2; megatrends, 23–32; methods of payment and, 2, 6, 8, 10–12, 42, 77; payment cards networks and, 37–38, 39;

payments industry and, 19, 20–21, 43–53; payments value chain and, 23; sunk investments, 48. *See also* Internet
Technologies: Android platform (Google), 30, 62, 70; "cloud-based computing," 13, 40–41, 65–68; contactless chip cards, 29, 64; digital check imaging, 26; electronic data capturing, 37–38; magnetic stripe cards, 37–38, 41, 42; modern computer systems, 40–41, 60; mobile/cell phone/wireless technology, 8, 12–13, 29–31, 32, 59, 60–65, 70, 108–09; M-Pesa, 63–64; online advertising, 57–60; Pay By Touch, 49–50; personalized e-coupons, 29; remote deposit capture, 26; search engines, 54; smart phones, 62; software platforms, 62, 67; virtual wallets, 29, 32
Tempo, 52–53, 75n33
TJX, 134–35
Transaction data, 53–60, 69, 70, 71
Transportation, 10–11, 31, 50–51
Trust. *See* Business issues

U.K. *See* United Kingdom
United Kingdom (U.K.), 31, 63
United States (U.S.): advertising industry in, 54; contactless payment systems in, 51; mass transit in, 31; mobile phones in, 63; payments industry in, 106–07; payments systems in, 8, 10, 20–21, 23, 25–26, 41, 42; use of cash and checks in, 107
USAA bank, 26
U.S. Mint, 20
U.S. Treasury, 20

Utilitarian perspectives, 80, 82

Verizon, 15, 106
Visa, 30, 32, 37, 75n48, 113, 119, 120, 130–31. *See also* Bank of America; Credit cards—specific

Walgreens, 51
Wells Fargo, 28–29

Wells, Henry, 103
Windows Mobile, 62
Wireless and mobile technologies. *See* Technologies

Xoom, 31

Yahoo!, 54
Yastremskiy, Maksym, 135